"If you want to write
the story of the Velvet
Underground, you have to
begin far beyond any of
the physical things that
actually happened. You
first have to look at New
York City, the mother which
spawned them, which gave
them its inner fire, creating
an umbilical attachment of
emotion to a monstrous hulk
of urban sprawl. You have to
walk its streets, ride its
subways, see it bustling and
alive in the day, cold and
haunted at night. And you
have to love it, embrace and
recognize its strange power,
for there, if anywhere, will
you find the roots."

—Lenny Kaye, *New Times*,
April 20, 1970

"ROCK AND ROLL CONSISTED OF JOEY DEE AND THE STARLIGHTERS, GUYS WHO PLAYED THE UPTOWN CLUBS AND HAD MATCHING SUITS. WE DIDN'T HAVE ANY OF THOSE THINGS SO WE HAD NO CHOICE WHATSOEVER OF WORKING ON THE MANHATTAN CLUB SCENE. THAT WAS BEYOND US, WE JUST COULDN'T DO IT, ANY MORE THAN WE COULD HAVE GONE TO LAS VEGAS."

—STERLING MORRISON

"OUR AIM WAS TO UPSET PEOPLE, MAKE THEM FEEL UNCOMFORTABLE,
MAKE THEM VOMIT."

—JOHN CALE

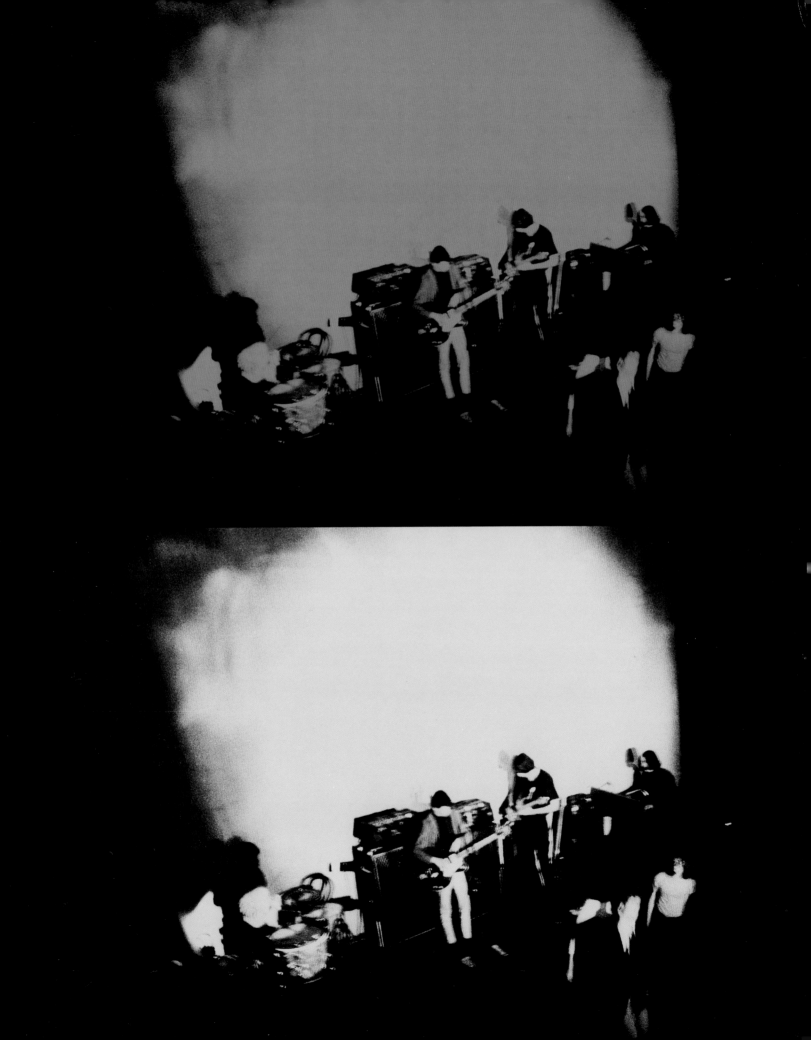

"Nothing could have prepared the kids and parents assembled in the auditorium for what they were about to experience that night. Everyone was hit by the screeching urge of sound, with a pounding beat louder than anything we'd ever heard."

—Rob Norris, reviewing the Velvets' first gig, at Summit High School, Summit, New Jersey, on December 11, 1965

"A THREE-RING PSYCHOSIS THAT ASSAULTS THE SENSES WITH THE SIGHTS AND SOUNDS OF THE TOTAL ENVIRONMENT SYNDROME."

—*VARIETY*, 1966

"The Velvet Underground has two styles of music. One is a phlegmatic mode which accompanies lyrics which smack of Baudelaire speaking through early-morning Bob Dylan; their other style is centered around a bone-scraping electric violin played by a boy who looks like a girl (their drummer is a girl who looks like a boy). The rumbling terror of their delivery is saved only by the viscous movement of the music: if it moves slowly enough, anything lethal becomes tolerable."

—Paul Jay Robbins, *Los Angeles Free Press*, May 13, 1966

"WARHOL'S SHOW [THE EXPLODING PLASTIC INEVITABLE] IS DECADENCE, CLEAN AS A GNAWED SKULL AND HONEST AS A CRAP IN THE CAN. IT IS ONLY AN EXTRUSION OF OUR NATIONAL DISEASE, OUR SOCIAL INSENSITIVITY. WE ARE A DYING CREATURE, AND WARHOL IS HOLDING OUR FAILING HAND AND SKETCHING THE CARCINOMA IN OUR SOUL."

—PAUL JAY ROBBINS, *LOS ANGELES FREE PRESS*, MAY 13, 1966

"The rock & roll music gets louder, the dancers get more frantic, and the lights start going on and off like crazy. And there are spotlights blinking in our eyes, and car horns beeping, and Gerard Malanga and the dancers are shaking like mad, and you don't think the noise can get any louder, and then it does, until there is one big rhythmic tidal wave of sound, pressing down around you, just impure enough so you can still get the beat; the audience, the dancers, the music and the movies, all of it fused together into one magnificent moment of hysteria."

—George English, review of the Exploding Plastic Inevitable at the Dom, *Fire Island News*, 1966

"WHAM! BAM! POW!!! NOT SINCE THE *TITANIC* RAN INTO THAT ICEBERG HAS THERE BEEN SUCH A COLLISION AS WHEN ANDY WARHOL'S EXPLODING PLASTIC INEVITABLE BURST UPON THE AUDIENCE AT THE TRIP . . ."

—KEVIN THOMAS, *LOS ANGELES TIMES*, MAY 5, 1966

"SOMETIMES THEY SING, SOMETIMES THEY JUST STROKE THEIR INSTRUMENTS INTO A SINGLE, HOUR-LONG JAM. THEIR SOUND IS A SAVAGE SERIES OF ATONAL THRUSTS AND ELECTRONIC FEEDBACK. THEIR LYRICS COMBINE SADO-MASOCHISTIC FRENZY WITH FREE-ASSOCIATION IMAGERY. THE WHOLE THING SEEMS TO BE THE PRODUCT OF A SECRET MARRIAGE BETWEEN BOB DYLAN AND THE MARQUIS DE SADE."

—RICHARD GOLDSTEIN, REVIEW OF SHOW AT THE BALLOON FARM, OCTOBER 1966

"The show is terrible. It goes on and on and on. . . . The light show is mediocre. The movies are long and boring—true Warhol. The Velvet Underground is totally unimpressive. Each one of their songs seems to last about three hours. . . ."

—Andrew Lugg and Larry Kasdan, EPI in Ann Arbor, *Michigan Daily*, November 4, 1967

"THEN: VELVET UNDERGROUND MINUS NICO BUT FEATURING A DRUMMER NAMED MAUREEN WHO BEATS THE SHIT OUT OF THE TOM-TOM AND THE BASS DRUM. HER HEAVY, CONTINUOUS 4/4 OUTPOURING ON THE DRUMS SLAMS INTO YOUR BOWELS AND CRAWLS OUT YOUR ASSHOLE. MEANWHILE, THE REST OF THE BAND MAKES A SOUND THAT CAN ONLY BE COMPARED TO A RAILROAD SHUNTING YARD, METAL WHEELS SCREECHING TO A HALT ON THE TRACKS. IT'S MUSIC TO GO OUT OF YOUR MIND TO, IF THAT'S YOUR BENT."

—ROBERT GOLD, SHRINE, *LOS ANGELES FREE PRESS*, JULY 26, 1968

"Let's not forget the noise. No one else could."

—Judy Altman, *Philadelphia Daily News*, December 12, 1966

"WARHOL HAS INDEED PUT TOGETHER A TOTAL ENVIRONMENT BUT IT IS AN ASSEMBLAGE THAT ACTUALLY VIBRATES WITH MENACE, CYNICISM AND PERVERSION. TO EXPERIENCE IT IS TO BE BRUTALIZED, HELPLESS—YOU'RE IN ANY KIND OF HORROR YOU WANT TO IMAGINE, FROM POLICE STATE TO MADHOUSE. EVENTUALLY THE REVERBERATIONS IN YOUR EARS STOP. BUT WHAT DO YOU DO WITH WHAT YOU STILL HEAR IN YOUR BRAIN? THE FLOWERS OF EVIL ARE IN FULL BLOOM WITH THE EXPLODING PLASTIC INEVITABLE."

—REVIEW OF THE EXPLODING PLASTIC INEVITABLE AT POOR RICHARD'S, *CHICAGO DAILY NEWS*, 1966

"Andy shows movies and we fuck dogs on stage"

—Lou Reed, quoted in Steven Watson's *Factory Made: Warhol and the Sixties*, 2003

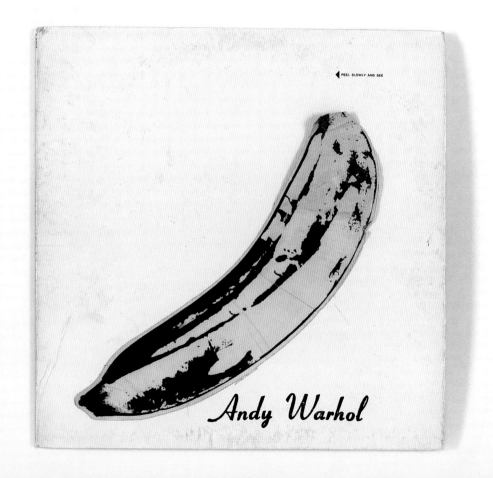

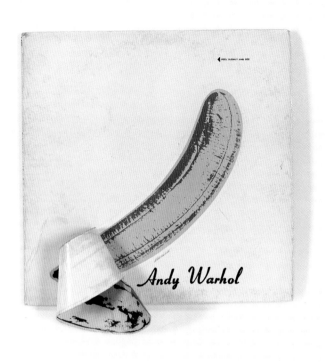

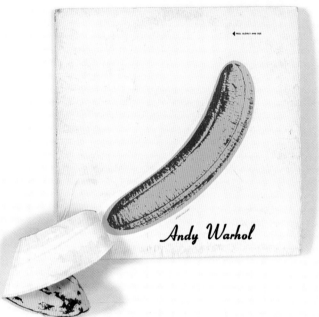

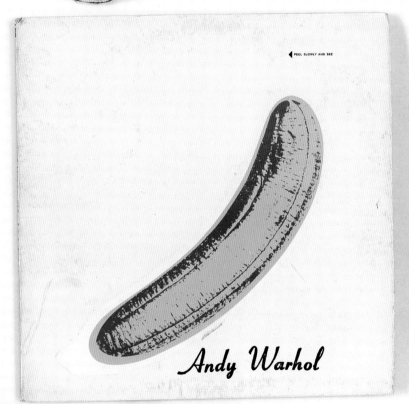

DO YOU WANT TO DANCE AND BLOW YOUR MIND WITH...

THE
VELVET
UNDERGROUND

★ ★

AN ILLUSTRATED
HISTORY
★ OF A WALK ON THE ★
WILDSIDE

★ ★

JIM DeROGATIS *with* BILL BENTLEY ★ GARTH CARTWRIGHT ★ NAT FINKELSTEIN ★ GLENN KENNY
GREG KOT ★ OLIVIER LANDEMAINE ★ LISA LAW ★ GERARD MALANGA ★ FRED W. MCDARRAH
BILLY NAME ★ ROB O'CONNOR ★ STEPHEN SHORE ★ DAVE SPRAGUE *and* **ANDY WARHOL**

VOYAGEUR PRESS

Pages 2–3: New York City skyline. *Hulton Archive/Getty Images*
Page 4: Joey Dee and the Starlighters. *Michael Ochs Archives/Getty Images*
Page 5: The Velvet Underground, Hollywood Hills, 1966. *Gerard Malanga*
Pages 6–7: Lit by Andy Warhol's light show, the Velvet Underground performs at the Gymnasium. *Billy Name/OvoWorks, Inc.*
Contents page: *Shutterstock*

DEDICATION

FOR LESTER BANGS, ROBERT QUINE, AND BRIAN ENO, FOR HELPING US TO UNDERSTAND AND
APPRECIATE THE IMPORTANCE OF THIS BAND, AS WELL AS FOR THE OTHER 4,997 PEOPLE WHO "GOT IT"
THE FIRST TIME AROUND

First published in 2009 by Voyageur Press, an imprint of MBI Publishing Company,
400 First Avenue North, Suite 300, Minneapolis, MN 55401 USA

Voyageur Press titles are also available at discounts in bulk quantity for industrial or sales-promotional use.
For details write to Special Sales Manager at MBI Publishing Company,
400 First Avenue North, Suite 300, Minneapolis, MN 55401 USA.

To find out more about our books, join us online at www.voyageurpress.com.

Library of Congress Cataloging-in-Publication Data

DeRogatis, Jim.
  The Velvet Underground : an illustrated history of a walk on the wild side / Jim DeRogatis with Bill Bentley ... [et al.].
     p. cm.
  Includes index.
  ISBN 978-0-7603-3672-4 (plc w/ band)
  1. Velvet Underground (Musical group) 2. Rock musicians--United
States--Biography. I. Bentley, Bill, 1950- II. Title.
  ML421.V44D47 2009
  782.42166092'2--dc22
  [B]
                                      2009006685

Editor: Michael Dregni
Design Manager: Katie Sonmor
Designer: John Barnett/4 Eyes Design

Printed in China

Credits:
Excerpts from *POPism: The Warhol Sixties* copyright © 1980 by Andy Warhol, reprinted by permission of Houghton Mifflin Harcourt
Publishing Company.

On the front cover: Velvet Underground band members from photographs by Gerard Malanga and MGM/Verve Records publicity;
used in a derivative work by permission, copyright © Gerard Malanga. Design by John Barnett/4 Eyes Design.

On the back cover: Velvets publicity photo and "Heroin" music. *Collection of The Andy Warhol Museum, Pittsburgh; Founding
Collection, Contribution The Andy Warhol Foundation for the Visual Arts, Inc.* Fillmore poster by artist Wes Wilson. Used by
permission, copyright © Wes Wilson. Other images from Voyageur Press collection.

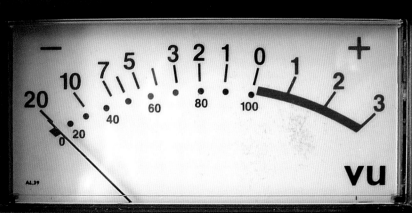

CONTENTS

THE SEMINAL VELVET UNDERGROUND

> "I have always believed that rock 'n' roll comes down to myth. There are no 'facts.'"
>
> —Lester Bangs, 1981

> "I REMEMBER WHEN THE VELVET UNDERGROUND CAME OUT, AND VERY FEW PEOPLE WERE INTERESTED IN THEM AT ALL. AND FOR A CERTAINTY I KNEW THAT THEY WERE GOING TO BECOME ONE OF THE MOST INTERESTING GROUPS, AND THAT THERE WOULD BE A TIME WHEN IT WOULDN'T BE THE BEATLES UP THERE AND THEN ALL THESE OTHER GROUPS DOWN THERE, IT WOULD BE A QUESTION OF ATTEMPTING TO ASSESS THE RELATIVE VALUES OF THE BEATLES AND THE VELVET UNDERGROUND AS EQUALS."
>
> —BRIAN ENO, *PUNK* MAGAZINE, 1976

> "Where does this album fit in?. . . I think it's great rock 'n' roll. I think Alexander the Great, Lord Byron, Jack the Ripper, F. Scott Fitzgerald, Albert Einstein, James Dean and other rock 'n' roll stars would agree with me."
>
> —Elliott Murphy, liner notes to *1969: The Velvet Underground Live with Lou Reed*

Such is the enduring influence of Lou Reed, John Cale, Sterling Morrison, and Maureen Tucker that it essentially has become a part of their collective name—they are *the Seminal Velvet Underground*, thank you very much—though in addition to standing as one of rock's hoariest clichés, that phrase also slights Tucker's role as one of rock's instrumental gender pioneers. Fine points like that hardly matter though in the mad competition to hyperbolize the band's genius. Witness another, even more resonant quote from that erudite musical philosopher Eno, though this one could be apocryphal (I've seen variations of it repeated dozens of times, but I've never found the original in any of his voluminous writings or interviews): "Only five thousand people ever bought a Velvet Underground album, but every single one of them started a band."

Mull that over for a second and you'll realize that it's pure hyperbole: All of those people can't possibly have formed bands, because many of them clearly became *rock critics*! Not to mention the fact that by now, we've endured many more than five thousand shameless Velvets clones and unapologetic VU namedroppers. But again, such distinctions don't seem to matter when so much praise has been heaped upon the band that new initiates and longtime fans alike both can be forgiven for thinking that the group descended from the heavens fully

Autographed Verve Records promotional photograph for *The Velvet Underground & Nico. Collection of The Andy Warhol Museum, Pittsburgh; Founding Collection, Contribution The Andy Warhol Foundation for the Visual Arts, Inc.*

Lou Reed

Sterling Morrison

John Cale

To Sweets - Love Mar

THE VELVET UNDERGROUND AND NICO **EXCLUSIVELY ON MGM/ VERVE RECORDS** R-1499

The early lineup of the Exploding Plastic Inevitable pose in the Silver Factory. Clockwise from top: Andy Warhol, Lou Reed, Nico, John Cale, Moe Tucker, dancer Mary Woronov, Sterling Morrison, dancer Gerard Malanga, and Nico's son, Ari Delon, the Factory's mascot.

formed, instantly brilliant, and utterly without peer—or, more appropriately as the case may be, that it emerged on the IRT direct from that other afterworld down below, with the musicians' foreboding black wardrobes and sheltering Ray-Bans still smoldering from the fire and brimstone they endured while forging their own Robert Johnson–style pact for musical immortality with the biggest, baddest Record Company Suit of all time (and I don't mean Jimmy Iovine).

Yes, this is exactly the sort of thing that Lester Bangs was getting at when he noted the power of myths in rock 'n' roll, and there is no bigger myth than that of *the Seminal Velvet Underground*. In truth, the VU myth was created in large part by Bangs himself as the band's most eloquent and prolific champion in print—though the late great rock critic also spent a considerable portion of his too-short career as the Boswell to Lou Reed's Samuel Johnson, trying to illuminate the facts that led to Reed's biggest artistic triumphs and most spectacular disasters as well as churning out thousands of words in the struggle to figure out what it all meant, only to conclude, not long before his death in 1982, that "Lou Reed is my own hero principally because he stands for all the most fucked-up things I could ever possibly conceive of—which probably only shows the limits of my imagination."

Poor Lester: He took it all so seriously—his was a life not only saved by rock 'n' roll but quite possibly also claimed by it. "Sometimes when people get obsessed with your work it's really dangerous for both of you," Reed told me when I asked him about Bangs in 1991. "You can disappoint someone like that so easily when they find out just how human you are."

True enough, but it also is true that an artist can inspire people even more when they realize that he or she fundamentally is just like them—not a god, not a genius, just another smart, talented, ambitious, but fucked-up kid from Long Island. That was a central theme for Andy Warhol throughout the 1960s: Anyone can be a Superstar, if only they have the desire (and if only for fifteen minutes). "The Pop idea was that anybody could do anything. So naturally, we're all trying to do it all," he said. It also is what punk rock began saying shortly after the Velvets, and what it has been saying ever since: Anybody can do it, if only they have the imagination.

In the end, knowing the facts doesn't cheapen the accomplishments of the Velvet Underground, it informs them, and knowing the context in which the group operated doesn't make it seem less unique, but more extraordinary, for being both a part of and a reaction against its times. Plus the facts make for a hell of a good story, and it begins, per the *Encyclopedia Britannica*, at Beth El Hospital in Brooklyn, New York, on March 2, 1942, with the birth of Lewis Alan Reed. 🕶

The Velvet Underground, reunited, 1993. *Renaud Monfourny/Courtesy Warner Bros. Records*

Chapter 1

FROM FREEPORT TO PICKWICK VIA SYRACUSE

"Then one fine mornin' she puts on a New York station
She couldn't believe what she heard at all
She started dancin' to that fine fine music
You know her life was saved by rock 'n' roll."

—Lou Reed, "Rock & Roll"

The man who would become simply Lou Reed was the first child born to Sidney George Rabinowitz, a New Yorker who anglicized his name and became a tax accountant, and the former Toby Futterman, a beauty queen turned housewife. The couple would have a second child, Elizabeth, better known as Bunny, when their son was five, and they would move their family from Brooklyn to the middle-class American-dream suburb of Freeport, Long Island, when Lewis was eleven. Like many Jewish mothers, Toby would dote on and sometimes smother her son, and like many Jewish fathers, Sid would goad and needle the boy with an acerbic sense of humor while fully expecting that he grow up to run the family business.

According to his biographers, the most prolific of whom has been the tireless Victor Bockris, Reed was subject to wild mood swings as a child, and these would continue throughout his life, to the point where those around him could never be sure which Lou Reed they'd be dealing with on a spectrum from warm and encouraging friend to cruel and egotistical bully. He attended Freeport High School, where he had a busy inner life filling notebooks with poetry and short stories, but where he also participated in sports, including track and field (specializing in running and pole vaulting) and basketball. Honing a theatrical rebellious streak, he convinced his parents to buy him a motorcycle, the better to emulate Marlon Brando in *The Wild One*. He became fascinated with Beat poetry and New York's underground gay culture ("I always thought that the one way kids had of getting back at their parents was to do this gender business: It was only kids trying to be outrageous," he said years later, when he seemed dedicated to erasing the history of his bisexuality). And he developed a lifelong obsession with rock 'n' roll, first as a devoted fan of the sounds coming over his AM radio at age twelve, and later as a budding guitarist playing with

Lou Reed in Andy Warhol's Silver Factory, circa 1966. *Stephen Shore* various ad hoc groups that performed at high school variety shows and odd gigs around town.

At sixteen Reed recorded some of the first songs he'd written with a combo called the Jades, and the aptly named single "So Blue" backed with "Leave Her For Me" was released in 1958 on the small Time Records label. "Our big moment came when [renowned New York DJ] Murray the K played it, but he was sick and someone else stood in," Reed recalled years later. "He played it once. I got royalties of seventy-eight cents. We were still in school. We'd open supermarkets, shopping centers, things like that. We had glitter jackets. It was what was called style—later on, people would call it punk, but at that time what we meant by punk was a pusher: 'He's just a fucking punk!'"

Troubled by his behavior, in 1959 Sid and Toby Reed followed the advice of a doctor and submitted their seventeen-year-old son to eight weeks of electro-shock therapy at Creedmore State Psychiatric Hospital, after which he entered therapy. It backfired: Lewis emerged even more resentful of his parents and convinced that he had to get as far away as possible to follow his own path. After briefly attending the uptown campus of New York University in the Bronx, he transferred upstate to the more distant Syracuse University, where he connected with the first of several difficult but inspiring mentors and surrogate fathers, the poet Delmore Schwartz,

Soundsville! was a Pickwick International creation from 1965 made up of songs co-authored by Lou Reed, who also sang many of the tunes and likely played guitar throughout.

"I went out and did the most horrifying things possible in those days. I joined a rock band. And, of course, I represented something very alien to my parents. I didn't have the bad ones [electro-shock treatments] where they don't put you to sleep first. I had the fun ones where they put you to sleep first. You count backwards, then you're out. It was shocking, but that's when I was getting interested in electricity anyway."

—Lou Reed, quoted in Victor Bockris and Gerard Malanga's *Up-Tight*, 1983

best known for his 1937 short story, "In Dreams Begin Responsibilities." Slowly drinking himself to death at Syracuse, Schwartz led Reed to believe that he could become a great writer, even though the student never showed the teacher any of his work.

Out Of Sight! featured Lou Reed's "Cycle Annie" by the Beachnuts with Reed on vocals and guitar.

At Syracuse Reed briefly hosted his own college radio show, spinning a mix of free jazz (heavy on the Ornette Coleman, Cecil Taylor, and Don Cherry) and R&B (favorites included James Brown and Hank Ballard). He also played in a series of bar bands that sometimes found him more interested in confronting the audience than in making them dance. In the process he made some soon-to-be fortuitous connections, meeting a likeminded guitarist named Sterling Morrison through their mutual friend Jim Tucker. Morrison reportedly was impressed that Reed used his electric guitar to blast screeching noise at the ROTC cadets marching on the green outside his dorm window.

In between classes Reed began to write gritty songs about life in the seedy underworld of Manhattan. He envisioned early versions of "I'm Waiting For The Man" and "Heroin" as the musical equivalent of what some of his favorite writers, Hubert Selby Jr. and Williams S. Burroughs, had done in *Last Exit to Brooklyn* and *Junky*.

Reed also wrote wickedly funny and twisted short stories, including one in which an obsessive lovesick "schmuck" mailed himself as a gift to his girlfriend studying in Wisconsin.

With a B.A. in hand Reed returned to his parents' house on Long Island in the summer of 1964, more determined than ever to devote his life to music. Instead of working for his father, he found a job as a house songwriter and staff musician with a cheap, exploitative record company called Pickwick International, a name chosen to enhance the mystique of its quickie British Invasion and Motown knock-offs. Among the songs Reed churned out in the label's no-frills recording studio were derivative tracks such as "Soul City," "Why Don't You Smile," "Tell Mama Not To Cry," and "Cycle Annie." Though he only held the job for five months, until February 1965, it looms large in his mythology: It brought a low-rent Brill Building discipline to his songwriting, and it provided the opportunity for him to meet John Cale.

Born in Garnant, South Wales, on March 9, 1942—a week after Reed was born in Brooklyn three thousand miles away—Cale's father was a coal miner, his mother a teacher and pianist. Though she failed to impress upon her son the importance of education—he hated school—his mother did instill a love of music, and this was further encouraged by his maternal uncles, one of whom hosted a radio show on the BBC and another of whom played violin. At thirteen Cale began a long association with the Welsh Youth Orchestra as a viola player, and some of those who heard him considered him a prodigy. Yet it was with the goal of fulfilling his mother's wishes that he enrolled in Goldsmiths' Teachers' College at the University of London in the fall of 1960.

In the end, Cale's college years sealed his fate of becoming a musician, since, like Reed with Schwartz, the young Welshman found a mentor: the radical intellectual Cornelius Cardew, who introduced him to the anti-art/anti-commercialism Fluxus Movement. The young viola player was fascinated by the work of John Cage and La Monte Young, classical avant-garde composers who were experimenting with minimalist repetition and atonal drones, and the enthusiastic young Welshman began to correspond with them and with another American composer he admired, Aaron Copland.

Interviewed and endorsed by Copland upon his graduation in London, Cale won a Leonard Bernstein scholarship to the Berkshire Music Center in Tanglewood, Massachusetts, bringing him one step closer to permanently escaping from Wales and moving to Manhattan. He made the most of Tanglewood, networking with another avant-garde giant, Yannis Xenakis; having his picture published in the *New York Times* when he was one of several pianists who performed Cage's eighteen-hour-plus epic "Vexations" in September 1963; and eventually linking up with Young's Theatre of Eternal Music, whose members included Terry Riley and Tony Conrad. (Cale and Conrad also formed an offshoot group called the Dream Syndicate.)

With Cage, Cale learned to embrace the unexpected. "He picked up the essential feeling I had that chaos isn't something to be afraid of. . . . His view was that if chaos

Before meeting Lou Reed, John Cale was playing with the Theatre of Eternal Music. The group performs here in a New York City loft, December 12, 1965. From left: American musician Tony Conrad, musician and composer La Monte Young, visual artist and musician Marion Zazeela, and Cale. *Fred W. McDarrah/Getty Images*

is the natural state of the universe, then we should accept that as it is, instead of trying to impose some sort of artificial regime on it," Cale wrote in his autobiography, *What's Welsh for Zen*. With Young and Conrad, he discovered that even the quest for the unexpected can be approached methodically. "The members of the Dream Syndicate, motivated by a scientific and mystical fascination with sound, spent long hours in rehearsals learning to provide sustained meditative drones and chants. Their rigorous style served to discipline me and developed my knowledge of the just intonation system. I also learned to use my viola in a new amplified way which would lead to the powerful droning effect that is so strong in the first two Velvet Underground records."

While working at Pickwick in early 1965, Reed stumbled across a fashion article about how ostrich feathers were all the rage. He quickly wrote a garage-rock stomper celebrating an invented dance craze called "The Ostrich" ("You bend forward, put your head between your knees/Do the ostrich, do the ostrich") that he recorded with a fictitious group called the Primitives.

Lou Reed's early single, "The Ostrich," by the Primitives, 1964.

"There were four of us literally locked in a room [at Pickwick] writing songs. They would say 'Write ten California songs, ten Detroit songs,' then we'd go down into the studio for an hour or two and cut three or four albums really quickly, which came in handy later because I knew my way around a studio, not well enough but I could work really fast. One day I was stoned and (after reading in Eugenia Sheppard's column that ostrich feathers were big that season) just for laughs—I decided to make up a dance. So I said, 'You put your head on the floor and have somebody step on it!' It was years ahead of its time."

—Lou Reed, quoted in Victor Bockris and Gerard Malanga's *Up-Tight*, 1983

One of Pickwick's owners, Terry Phillips, thought it could be a hit, and he set out to find musicians to join Reed in a group to promote the single. Cale, Conrad, and their friend Walter De Maria agreed to take the gig as a lark and were shocked to discover that a key ingredient of the song was what Reed called "Ostrich guitar," which featured all six strings tuned to the same note—a primitive, rock 'n' roll version of what they were doing with more structure and classical instrumentation in the Dream Syndicate and the Theatre of Eternal Music.

When "The Ostrich" failed to dent the pop charts, the Primitives' gigs dried up after a few weekend appearances, and Pickwick moved on to the next piece of product in the pipeline. But a friendship endured between Reed and Cale, and they began to collaborate in the latter's flat in a slum on Ludlow Street in the Lower East Side. Reed was struck by Cale's musicianship, and Cale admired Reed's ability to improvise lyrics, but it's an unfair if popular simplification to say that the Welsh prodigy brought virtuosity and sophisticated avant-garde ideas to the Long Islander's raw rock 'n' roll. Reed already was an accomplished musician in his own right and a voracious student of adventurous sounds ranging from free-form jazz to Karlheinz Stockhausen, and though Cale hadn't played much rock 'n' roll professionally, he had been gripped by its power since he first heard Elvis Presley as a teenager listening to the BBC. Now he began to help Reed rewrite Syracuse-era songs such as "Heroin" and "I'm Waiting For The Man," alternating between amplified viola and electric bass as needed, as well as developing new material such as "The Black Angel's Death Song."

Cale soon left the classical world behind, and he never looked back. "It was the time of the Beatles," he wrote. "I stopped working with La Monte and dove into working with Lou."

To complete their nascent band, Reed recruited Sterling Morrison on second guitar after he'd happened upon his old acquaintance from Syracuse during a chance meeting in the New York subway, and Cale turned to his neighbor, drummer Angus MacLise, who sometimes played hand drums with the Theatre of Eternal Music. The quartet began to do odd gigs, including several at the Café Wha?, first under the name the Falling Spikes, then for a while as the Warlocks (coincidentally, the same name chosen by an early version of the Grateful Dead). One day Conrad visited carrying a tawdry paperback he found on the street about sadomasochistic sex called *The Velvet Underground*. That was the name that finally stuck. "It's the funniest dirty book I've ever read," Reed said a few years later, in a 1969 interview with *Open City*. "'Into the murky depths of depravity and debauchery with the Velvet Underground. . . .' This is too good! I mean, just the name: I love the ring of it."

In July 1965, the Velvet Underground recorded a demo that included "Heroin," "Venus In Furs," "The Black

The first incarnation of the Velvet Underground, 1965. From left: John Cale, Angus MacLise, Sterling Morrison, and Lou Reed. *Donald Greenhaus/Shabobba International*

Angel's Death Song," and "Wrap Your Troubles In Dreams." Inspired by some of the adventurous recordings that Cale had recently brought back from a visit to the United Kingdom, including records by the Who and the Kinks, the group thought it might be able to find a home with a label in the United States. It was all getting to be a bit too crass and commercial for the mystical purist MacLise, who disliked the ideas of being paid to play music or of having to show up, start, and stop at preordained times. He quit the group, but the problem of his departure quickly was solved when Morrison and Reed turned to the younger sister of their old Syracuse buddy Jim Tucker.

Reed, Cale, Morrison, and Maureen Tucker played their first gig together at Summit High School, twenty-five miles from Manhattan in Summit, New Jersey, on December 11, 1965, sandwiched between two long-forgotten groups called 40 Fingers and the Myddle Class, earning seventy-five dollars for their troubles. As chance would have it the audience included a student who, several years later, would perform in the Doug Yule–led version of the band during its last European tour in 1972, as well as going on to further recognition with the power-pop band the Bongos, though at the time Rob Norris was just another suburban kid who had his mind blown.

"Nothing could have prepared the kids and parents assembled in the auditorium for what they were about to experience that night," Norris recalled. "Everyone was hit by the screeching urge of sound, with a pounding beat louder than anything we'd ever heard." Shortly into "Heroin," the second song, "most of the audience retreated in horror for the safety of their homes, thoroughly convinced of the dangers of rock 'n' roll music."

"I am simply a man who found himself by accident, and unhappily at times, in a strange and alien world, or, rather, an unreal and unquiet underworld, and who reported on it—that and no more."

—Michael Leigh, *The Velvet Underground*, 1963

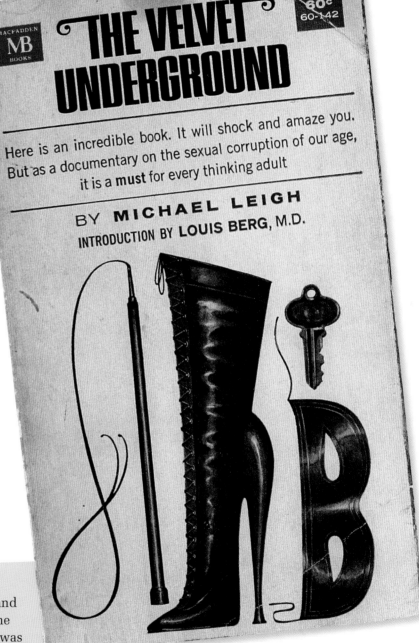

THE VELVET UNDERGROUND

60¢
60-142

MACFADDEN MB BOOKS

Here is an incredible book. It will shock and amaze you. But as a documentary on the sexual corruption of our age, it is a **must** for every thinking adult

BY **MICHAEL LEIGH**

INTRODUCTION BY **LOUIS BERG**, M.D.

"We had a name at last! And it was adopted by us and deemed appropriate not because of the S&M theme of the book, but because the word 'underground' was suggestive of our involvement in the underground film and art scenes."

—Sterling Morrison, quoted in Victor Bockris and Gerard Malanga's *Up-Tight*, 1983

The book that gave a band its name: Michael Leigh's report on "the sexual corruption of our age," *The Velvet Underground*, 1963.

CBS News filmed *The Making of an Underground Film* in November 1965 documenting the creation of filmmaker Piero Heliczer's *Venus In Furs* movie. Lou Reed, Sterling Morrison, and John Cale—along with Heliczer on saxophone—covered themselves in ghostly white makeup to perform "Heroin."
Adam Ritchie/Redferns

Photo by John E. Lynch

the myddle class

IN CONCERT

Summit High School Auditorium
125 Kent Place Blvd. Summit, N. J.

8 p.m.   December 11, 1965   Admission: $2.50

Tickets may be purchased in advance at:

Scotti's Record Shop	Adams Haberdashers	Henriksen's Pharmacy
346 Springfield Ave.	1271 Springfield Ave.	415 Springfield Ave.
Summit	New Providence	Berkeley Heights

Tickets may also be purchased in advance by sending a check or money order to
the myddle class, Box 221, Berkeley Heights, N. J.

Also appearing on the program:

The Forty Fingers   **The Velvet Underground**

"At Summit we opened with 'There She Goes Again,' then played 'Venus In Furs,' and ended with 'Heroin.' The murmur of surprise that greeted our appearance as the curtain went up increased to a roar of disbelief once we started to play 'Venus,' and swelled to a mighty howl of outrage and bewilderment by the end of 'Heroin.' Al Aronowitz observed that we seemed to have an oddly stimulating and polarizing effect on audiences."

—Sterling Morrison, 1983

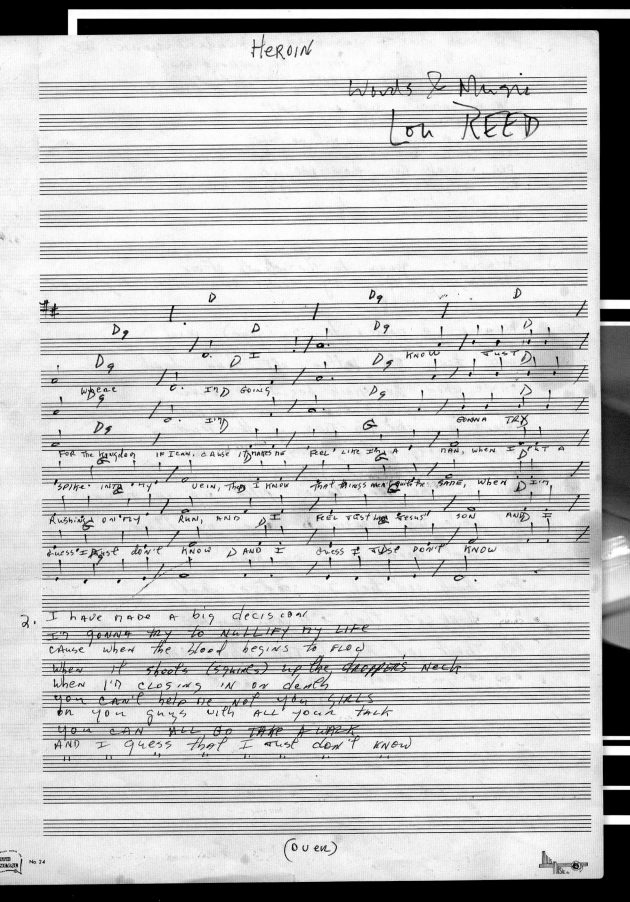

Chapter 2

ANDY AND THE BANANA ALBUM

"This is a rock group called the Velvet Underground
I show movies on them
Do you like their sound?
'Cause they have a style that grates and I have art to make."

—Lou Reed and John Cale,
"The Style It Takes" from *Songs For Drella*, 1990

Given how familiar rock fans have become with the larger-than-life personas they've created over the last five decades, it's not hard to imagine how Lou Reed and John Cale could easily have slid into the legendarily vibrant, colorful, perverse, and intensely competitive scene that surrounded Andy Warhol at the Factory in 1966. In their mid-twenties, both musicians possessed boundless talent, prodigious intellects, intense sexual magnetism, and the skills for living on the edge and pushing other people's buttons, even if they still were privately wracked with insecurities. It's more difficult to envision the other two members of the Velvet Underground as Warhol Superstars, though that's really more of a compliment than a put-down.

Reed's new bandmates both were born less than ten miles from his family's house in Freeport: Holmes Sterling Morrison Jr. on August 28, 1942, in East Meadow; and Maureen Ann Tucker on August 26, 1944,

in Levittown. Morrison's parents divorced when he was young, and he became a bright, talented, and sarcastic teen obsessed with music, mastering first the trumpet and then the electric guitar. "I graduated high school with very high numbers and matching low esteem, for just about everything but music," he said. With the Velvet Underground he and Reed often alternated on lead and rhythm guitar, and though he disliked it, Morrison also played bass when Cale moved to organ or viola. Precise and powerful, Morrison's rhythm guitar provided the solid foundation for Reed's noisier free-form excursions, while his leads added the gorgeous melodic filigree that Reed never seemed to have the patience to craft on the quieter songs. "When he had played his passionate solos, I had always seen him as a mythic Irish hero, flames shooting from his nostrils," Reed said of Morrison in the *New York Times Magazine*. "[He was] the warrior heart of the Velvet Underground."

John Cale and Lou Reed perform at Greenwich Village's Café Bizarre, the venue where Andy Warhol first saw the band, in December 1965. *Adam Ritchie /Redferns*

For her part, Tucker's interest in the drums began in 1962, when she was seventeen. "I was in the high school library when an announcement came over: 'Anyone who would like to sell candy to help pay for an African drummer named [Babatunde] Olatunji to come to assembly to play, please go to the office,'" she recalled in an interview with Jason Gross of the webzine *Perfect Sound Forever*. "I *ran* to the office for that! So, in our silly little Levittown school, we got Olatunji and his full troop with ten or twelve musicians and ten or twelve dancers, and it was just stunning."

Tucker began playing the drums herself at age nineteen, strictly for her own amusement while studying at Ithaca College, and she was practicing in her bedroom at night after working for IBM as a keypunch operator during

> **"There are two kinds of drummers—Moe Tucker and everybody else."**
>
> **—Lou Reed**

the day when she first heard from Reed asking her to temporarily fill in for a gig in New Jersey. She took the job and stayed. As she stood wielding her tympani mallets on a snare drum and a bass drum set on its side, largely eschewing cymbals, she brought both an enigmatic presence to the group—many concertgoers couldn't figure out if she was a boy or a girl—and a primal and relentless

[*continued on 42*]

For the Café Bizarre's tourists, the Velvet Underground was too outré, too shocking, and just plain too loud. The café manager forced Maureen Tucker to forego her bass drum and just tap a tambourine. In the end, the band members played their "The Black Angel's Death Song" one too many times and were fired. Andy Warhol was impressed. *Adam Ritchie/Redferns*

"The moral of
the tale is this:
Whoever allows himself
to be whipped,
deserves to be whipped."

—Leopold von Sacher-Masoch,
Venus in Furs, 1870

"The Bizarre management
wasn't too thrilled with
them. Their music was
beyond the pale—way too
loud and insane for any
tourist coffeehouse clientele.
People would leave looking
dazed and damaged."

—Andy Warhol,
POPism, 1980

"S&M sex fascinated me even
though I knew nothing about
it. I had a natural curiosity, so I
asked Lou, 'What's "Venus In Furs"
about?' Lou said, 'Ah, you know, it's
some trash novel.' I said, 'Where can
I get a copy?' Lou said, 'Ah, yeah, just
down the block there's a store.' So I
went and bought the book. I was still
in high school, so I'd go to class with
my *Venus in Furs* and *Story of O* and
Justine, and sit there reading this stuff."

—Ronnie Cutrone, Exploding Plastic Inevitable
dancer, quoted in Legs McNeil and Gillian
McCain's *Please Kill Me*, 1996

"Don't you know me yet? Yes, I am cruel—
since you take so much delight in that
word—and am I not entitled to be so? Man
is the one who desires; woman the one
who is desired. This is woman's entire, but
decisive, advantage. Through his passion
nature has given man into woman's hands,
and the woman who does not know how
to make him her subject, her slave, her toy,
and how to betray him with a smile in the
end is not wise."

—Leopold von Sacher-Masoch,
Venus in Furs, 1870

The book that inspired one of the band's most famous songs: nineteenth-century Austrian author Leopold von
Sacher-Masoch's erotic novel *Venus in Furs*. Masoch's name inspired the term "masochism."

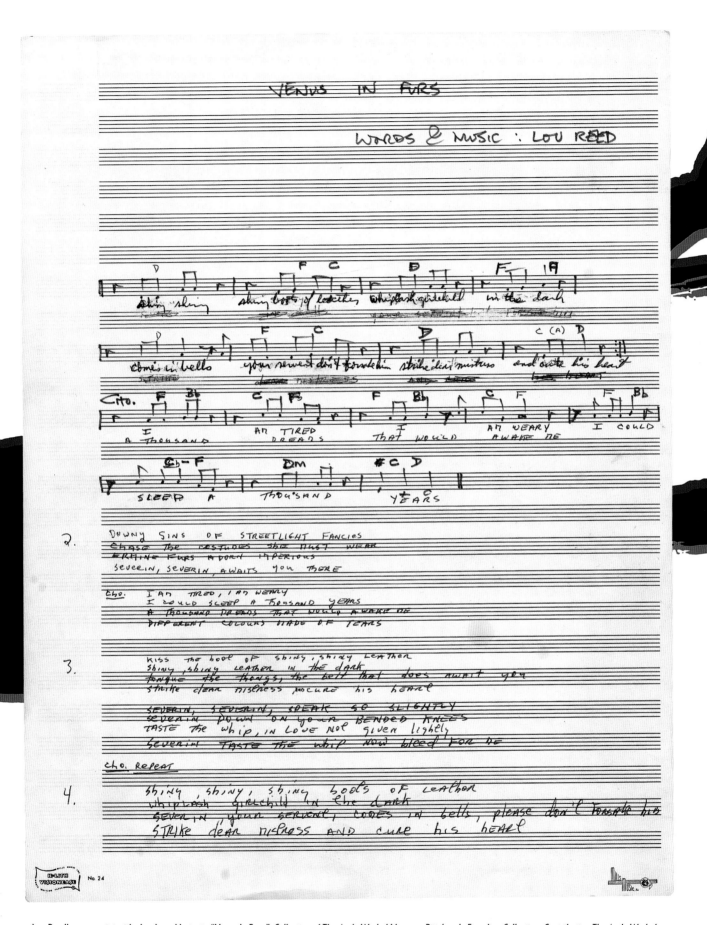

Lou Reed's manuscript with chords and lyrics to "Venus In Furs." *Collection of The Andy Warhol Museum, Pittsburgh; Founding Collection, Contribution The Andy Warhol Foundation for the Visual Arts, Inc.*

[continued from 39]

backbeat that came straight from Africa via two of her rock 'n' roll idols, Bo Diddley and Charlie Watts.

On December 15, 1965, four days after their less-than-illustrious gig at Summit High School, Reed, Cale, Morrison, and Tucker began a two-week residency at a Greenwich Village tourist trap called the Café Bizarre. They needed the experience onstage, not to mention the money, but the former was tainted by the fact that Tucker had to play tambourine because the club owner said her drums were too loud, and the latter was meager indeed. The sets included all of the originals they'd written to date, as well as time-killing covers by Jimmy Reed and Chuck Berry.

Early in the run the Velvets played a show for an audience that included Paul Morrissey and Gerard Malanga, Andy Warhol's left- and right-hand men at the Factory, who were charged at the time with finding a band to perform at a discotheque that the pop artist was considering endorsing and using as a showcase for his movies, his art, and the fascinating people that he enjoyed collecting, manipulating, and using as a source of energy and inspiration. (Not for nothing was his nickname Drella, a contraction of Dracula and Cinderella.) As coincidence would have it, Warhol had dabbled with sponsoring a rock band once before, in 1963, but the project—which featured La Monte Young and Walter De Maria, Cale's old cohorts in the Theatre of Eternal Music—never amounted to much.

Now Malanga liked the Velvets so much that he twirled around the dance floor cracking the bull whip he carried to accessorize his black leather ensemble, and he and Morrissey soon returned with Warhol and his then-reigning Superstar, Edie Sedgwick. The legend holds that they caught the band's last show at the venue:

Andy Warhol's new rock band rehearses for the first time at the Silver Factory, circa late 1965 through early 1966. *Nat Finkelstein*

The club owner warned the group not to perform its dissonant version of "The Black Angel's Death Song" again, whereupon the musicians promptly played it once more and were fired. True or not, it was exactly the sort of spirit Warhol admired.

Since his first solo Pop-Art exhibit in Manhattan, in November 1962, Warhol had become the single most discussed name in the New York art world, polarizing people with his repetitive images of Marilyn Monroe, Campbell's Soup cans, and Coca-Cola bottles, as well as his "sculptures" of Brillo boxes. Working out of the aluminum foil–lined loft in a building on East 47th Street that would become known as the Silver Factory, he began making films in 1963 with the somnambulistic *Sleep*; two years later he'd become so enamored of moviemaking that he'd announced he was retiring from painting. That didn't last

long, but at age thirty-six, Warhol clearly was growing restless and looking for new ways to express himself—he also made the tape recordings that would become the basis for *a: a novel* at this time. The Velvet Underground entered his orbit at exactly the right moment. "It was like bang! They were with Andy and Andy was with them and they backed him absolutely. They would have walked to the end of the earth for him. And that happened in one day!" actress, dancer, and Factory regular Mary Woronov recalled.

On New Year's Eve, 1965–1966, the Velvets could be heard performing "Heroin" on a CBS-TV news report called "The Making of an Underground Film" spotlighting director Piero Heliczer and narrated by Walter Cronkite; meanwhile Warhol, Sedgwick, Malanga, and several members of the band headed to the Apollo Theater in Harlem to see James Brown.

[continued on 46]

A member of New York City's finest turns down the volume on the Velvets' Vox amp head during a rehearsal at Andy Warhol's Silver Factory. It wasn't the first time the band's sound was deemed too loud—nor would it be the last. *Stephen Shore*

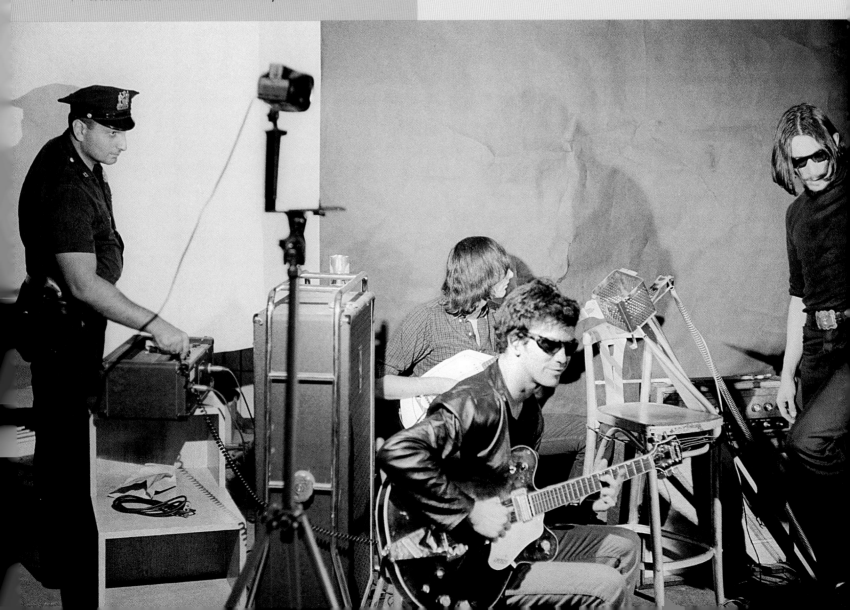

The Exploding Plastic Inevitable and miscellaneous other Warhol Superstars pose surrounding Edie Sedgwick (on the couch back) for Factory photographer Nat Finkelstein. The group was filming Andy Warhol's movie *Lupe* at Panna Grady's apartment. Back row from left: "manager" Paul Morrissey, EPI sound- and lightman Danny Williams, Warhol, Lou Reed, Sterling Morrison, John Cale, dancer Gerard Malanga, and Barbara Rubin (half hidden). Front row: Jason Collins, Shirley Lark, Martha Dargan (turned away), and film critic Donald Lyons.
Nat Finkelstein

Andy Warhol was invited to speak at the New York Society for Clinical Psychiatry's annual dinner at Delmonico's Hotel, Manhattan, on January 13, 1966. He brought with him his fledgling multimedia freak show, including his new band. The Velvet Underground's rock 'n' roll was an electric shock to the black-tie guests. *Adam Ritchie/Redferns*

[*continued from 43*]

Less than two weeks later, on January 13, 1966, Warhol brought the Velvets along to a speaking engagement before the New York Society for Clinical Psychiatry at Delmonico's Hotel. The *New York Times* reported on the gathering the next day under the headline "Syndromes Pop at Delmonico's": "There was John Cale, leader of the Velvet Underground, in a black suit with rhinestones on the collar. There was Nico, identified by Warhol as 'a famous fashion model and now a singer,' in a white slack suit with long blond hair. And there were all those psychiatrists," reporter Grace Glueck wrote. "The

act really came into its own about midway through the dinner (roast beef with string beans and small potatoes) when the Velvet Underground swung into action. The high-decibel sound, aptly described by Dr. Campbell as 'a short-lived torture of cacophony,' was a combination of rock 'n' roll and Egyptian belly-dance music." (No doubt any joy that Reed got from torturing the psychiatrists— payback for what they'd put him through as a teen—was mitigated when he read the review and learned that Cale was the leader of *his* band, to say nothing of the odd nod to belly-dancing.)

"Why they asked us to play [at the Annual Dinner of the New York Society for Clinical Psychiatry], I have no idea—two hundred psychiatrists and us, these freaks from the Factory. Afterwards people like Gerard [Malanga] and Barbara Rubin just carried on with their tape recorders and cameras, going to tables and asking these ridiculous questions. People were flabbergasted. I just sort of sat back and said, 'What the hell are we doing here?' Then I realized maybe the shrinks thought they'd take notes or something."

—Maureen Tucker, quoted in Legs McNeil and Gillian McCain's *Please Kill Me*, 1996

"We were in it for the exaltation and could not be swayed from our course to do it exactly as we wanted."

—John Cale, quoted in Steven Watson's *Factory Made: Warhol and the Sixties*, 2003

The Velvets' association with Warhol would prove to be both a blessing—as the *New York Times*' coverage of a group barely two months old illustrates, it brought instant notoriety—and a curse, since it also subjected the band to instant stereotyping as "just another Warhol gimmick." In the beginning, though, it was all good, and it all happened very, very quickly—not surprising, considering that the scene largely was fueled by the prodigious consumption of speed. By February, Warhol had shot the band rehearsing at the Factory for a film called *Symphony of Sound*; the group had provided the soundtrack for two more of his movies, *Hedy* and *More Milk Yvette*, and it had begun performing in front of Warhol's movies and behind some of the flamboyant dancers from the Factory in a multimedia show called *Andy Warhol, Up-Tight*, staged nightly at the underground film center Cinémathèque. But as the *Times* review indicated, Warhol's biggest contribution to the band came via the addition of a chanteuse.

Most likely born in Cologne, Germany, in 1938, Christa Päffgen left school at thirteen and began selling lingerie, which led to some modeling jobs in Berlin. From there she moved to Paris and fashion spreads in *Vogue*, *Tempo*, and *Elle* through the late 1950s; she also did a number of small film roles, most notably in Federico Fellini's *La Dolce Vita*, released in 1959. By that time she'd adopted the name Nico, inspired by photographer Herbert Tobias while on a modeling assignment in Ibiza.

Advertisement from the *Village Voice* for *Andy Warhol, Up-Tight* at the Film-Makers' Cinemathèque, February 8-13, 1966, featuring the band plus Superstar Edie Sedgwick and dancer-poet Gerard Malanga along with Warhol.

Jetting between Paris, New York, and London through the early 1960s, Nico made her first foray into rock 'n' roll in 1965 when she met Brian Jones of the Rolling Stones and recorded a single, "I'm Not Sayin'," for Andrew Loog Oldham's Immediate Records label. A few months later she met Bob Dylan, who reportedly wrote "I'll Keep It With Mine" for her. In January 1966 she moved to New York and quickly became a Factory regular and a member of the Velvet Underground.

Nico sings for the *Up-Tight* performance at the Film-Makers' Cinemathèque on February 8, 1966. *Fred W. McDarrah/Getty Images*

"[NICO] LOOKED LIKE SHE COULD HAVE MADE THE TRIP OVER RIGHT AT THE FRONT OF A VIKING SHIP, SHE HAD THAT KIND OF FACE AND BODY."

—ANDY WARHOL, QUOTED IN STEVEN WATSON'S *FACTORY MADE: WARHOL AND THE SIXTIES*, 2003

THE RUTGERS FILM SOCIETY
PRESENTS

ANDY WARHOL'S
"UNDERGROUND NEW YORK"
FEATURING TWO FILMS IN COLOR & DOUBLE SCREEN

"VINYL"
Starring Gerard Malanga & Edith Sedgwick
WRITTEN BY RONNIE TAVEL

"LUPE"
Starring Edith Sedgwick & Billy Linich

PLUS ON STAGE

THE VELVET UNDERGROUND
AND
NICO

"RUTGERS UPTIGHT"
TO BE FILMED IN AUDIENCE
WITH
Andy Warhol, Edith Sedgwick, Nico, Barbara Rubin, Gerard Malanga
Danny Williams, Billy Linich, Paul Morrissey, the Velvet Underground

WEDNESDAY MARCH 9th
AT 8:00 & 10:00

SCOTT HALL

ALL SEATS $2.00

TICKETS ON SALE AT LEDGE, COMMONS & T. S. MEM   RS

Poster, Rutgers Uptight, Rutgers University, New Brunswick, New Jersey, March 9, 1966. *Collection of The Andy Warhol Museum, Pittsburgh; Founding Collection, Contribution The Andy Warhol Foundation for the Visual Arts, Inc.*

"The group needed something beautiful to counteract the kind of screeching ugliness they were trying to sell, and the combination of a really beautiful girl standing in front of all this decadence was what was needed."

—Paul Morrissey, quoted in Victor Bockris and Gerard Malanga's *Up-Tight*, 1983

The Velvets had been wary of the idea of having "a chick in the band": At first Cale even balked at the asexual Tucker, mindful perhaps of the two abortive attempts that he and Reed had made to work with female singers in their earliest days as the Warlocks and the Falling Spikes. The group compromised to a point—Nico was given a few lead vocals but spent much of her time on stage banging a tambourine—because, well, Warhol wanted it that way, and because Reed and Cale soon fell under her spell. (During her brief time with the group she had romantic entanglements with both of them.) But there is no denying that she was a fascinating presence visually and musically. "Half goddess, half icicle," pioneering rock critic Richard Goldstein wrote in the *Village Voice*. "She sings in perfect mellow ovals. It sounds something like a cello getting up in the morning."

Shortly after they met, Reed wrote two of the Velvet Underground's most beautiful songs with Nico's voice in mind: "Femme Fatale," based on a suggestion by Warhol that he pen a tune about Sedgwick, and "I'll Be Your Mirror." These provided the moments of unsettling calm in the otherwise tumultuous assault of the band's live shows, which Warhol took on the road in March to a number of college art departments, including Rutgers University in New Brunswick, New Jersey, and the University of Michigan in Ann Arbor. "If they can take it for ten minutes, then we play it for fifteen," Warhol wrote. "That's our policy: Always leave them wanting less."

Lou Reed and Andy Warhol hang out at the Silver Factory. *Stephen Shore*

On the banner:
ANDY
WARHOL

LIVE

THE
VELVET
UNDER-
GROUND

LIVE
DANCING

FILMS

PARTY
EVENT
NOW

POLSKI DOM NARODOWY

POLSKI DOM NARODOWY

The Dom

BAR   The Dom   23

Andy Warhol and Paul Morrissey rented the Dom (shortened from *Polski Dom Narodowy*, or "Polish National Home") at 23 St. Mark's Place in the East Village to showcase the Exploding Plastic Inevitable, April 1–30, 1966. *Fred W. McDarrah/Getty Images*

OPEN STAGE

23 ST. MARKS PLACE (Bet. 2nd & 3rd Aves.)

NIGHTLY · 9 PM TO 2 AM

EXPLODING   PLASTIC

INEVITABLE

LIVE!

ANDY WARHOL

THE

VELVET UNDERGROUND

AND

NICO

MUSIC! MOVIES! DANCING! MORE MOVIES!

Gerard MALANGA · Mary WORONOV

ON FILM – ON STAGE – ON VINYL

LIGHTWORKS   VISIONS   ULTRASOUNDS

NO MINIMUM

MURRAY POSTER PRINTING Co. Inc., 221 W. 64 St. NYC

The following month the focus was back on New York as Warhol rented a Polish dance hall on St. Mark's Place—*Polsky Dom Narodny*, or "the Dom" for short—to host the multimedia assault of film, dance, lights, and music that he now called the Exploding Plastic Inevitable. This run coincided with a show at Leo Castelli's gallery featuring his cow wallpaper and floating silver "cloud" pillows. It seemed as if the pop artist could do no wrong, and with a cover charge of six dollars, the Dom engagement netted eighteen thousand in its first week, though Factory overseer Morrissey only paid each of the Velvets five bucks a day.

While the Dom run was still going on, Warhol used some of the money, augmented by an investment from former Columbia Records sales executive Norman Dolph, to put the Velvet Underground into the run-down Scepter Recording Studio on West 54th Street. Dolph and John Licata engineered the sessions, which were contentious and nerve-wrangling, since nobody really knew what they were doing. Nevertheless, four days of recording and mixing yielded the versions of "Femme Fatale," "Run Run Run," "All Tomorrow's Parties," "There She Goes Again," "I'll Be Your Mirror," "The Black Angel's Death Song," and "European Son" that eventually appeared on the band's debut album. Then it was back on the road again as Warhol took the Exploding Plastic Inevitable to California in May 1966.

[continued on 57]

DO YOU WANT TO DANCE AND BLOW YOUR MIND WITH

THE EXPLODING PLASTIC INEVITABLE

live

ANDY WARHOL

THE VELVET UNDERGROUND

and

NICO

Superstars Gerard Malanga And Mary Woronov On Film On Stage On Vinyl
LIVE MUSIC, DANCING, ULTRA SOUNDS, VISIONS, LIGHTWORKS BY DANIEL WILLIAMS, COLOR SLIDES BY JACKIE CASSEN, DISCOTHEQUE, REFRESHMENTS, INGRID SUPERSTAR, FOOD, CELEBRITIES AND MOVIES INCLUDING: VINYL, SLEEP, EAT, KISS, EMPIRE, WHIPS, FACES, HARLOT, HEDY, COUCH, BANANA, ETC, ETC, ETC. ALL IN THE SAME PLACE AT THE SAME TIME.

FIRST COME FIRST SERVED. OCCUPANCY BY MORE THAN 750 PEOPLE IS CONSIDERED UNLAWFUL. PROGRAM REPEATED SATURDAY APRIL 9TH 3 PM, FOR TEENAGE TOT AND TILLIE DROPOUT DANCE MARATHON MATINEE. $1.00

AT THE OPEN STAGE 23 ST. MARK'S PLACE (BET. 2ND & 3RD AVES.) 9-2 NITELY

NO MINIMUM, WEEKNIGHTS $2.00, FRIDAY AND SATURDAY $2.50   674-9742

Edie Sedgwick and Gerard Malanga dance as part of the Exploding Plastic Inevitable show at the Dom.
Nat Finkelstein

Andy Warhol's New York City cabaret card, issued March 31, 1966.
Collection of The Andy Warhol Museum, Pittsburgh; Founding Collection,
Contribution The Andy Warhol Foundation for the Visual Arts, Inc.

Sketch of the Exploding Plastic Inevitable performing at the Dom on April 1, 1966, including "Lois (LuLu)" Reed, Nico, John Cale, Mo "you piece of shit" Tucker, "Stella" (Sterling Morrison), and Andy Warhol in the projection booth. The drawing is attributed to Ingrid Superstar. *Collection of The Andy Warhol Museum, Pittsburgh; Founding Collection, Contribution The Andy Warhol Foundation for the Visual Arts, Inc.*

"I had to come up with a name for the show—the lights and the dancers that went with the Velvet Underground and Nico, and I was looking at this stupid Dylan album that had always intrigued me a bit, I don't know which one it was, but I seem to recall there's a picture of Barbara Rubin on the back [*Bringing It All Back Home*, although the inspiration likely came from *Highway 61 Revisited* liner notes]. So I was looking at the gibberish that was typed on the back, and I said, 'Look, use the word "exploding," something "plastic," and whatever that means, "inevitable".'"

—Paul Morrissey, Exploding Plastic Inevitable "manager," quoted in Legs McNeil and Gillian McCain's *Please Kill Me*, 1996

John Cale plays on his electric bass at the Dom performances. *Nat Finkelstein*

"Let 'em sing about going steady on
the radio. Let the campus types run
hootenannies. But it's in holes like this
that the real stuff is being born."

—Lou Reed, quoted during an Exploding
Plastic Inevitable show at the Dom, 1966

Nico in her white suit fronts the Exploding Plastic Inevitable at the Dom. *Billy Name/OvoWorks, Inc.*

"With every show we were coming more alive, like Frankenstein's
monster discovering that it could walk"

—John Cale, quoted in Steven Watson's *Factory Made: Warhol and
the Sixties*, 2003

ANDY WARHOL

presents the PLASTIC INEVITABLE SHOW with

Newsweek

APRIL 25, 1966 40c

POP!

THE VELVET UNDERGROUND [and] NICO chanteuse & light shows & curious movies

MAY 3-18

NEW SHRINE OF POP CULTURE

TRIP
8572 sunset strip
call 652-4600

[continued from 51]

At the time the West Coast scene epitomized everything the Velvets disdained in popular music and culture. Morrison put it most succinctly: "We all hated hippies," he said, and they sneered at the music they'd heard by the Jefferson Airplane, Frank Zappa, and the Grateful Dead. At least one of the key voices behind the flower-power hype returned that animosity: "Warhol's Exploding Plastic Inevitable was nothing more than a condensation of all the bum trips of the Trips Festival," wrote Ralph J. Gleason, music critic for the *San Francisco Chronicle* and an early mentor to Jann Wenner as he started *Rolling Stone*. "It was all very campy and very Greenwich Village sick. If this is what America's waiting for, we are going to die of boredom because this is a celebration of the silliness of café society, way out in left field instead of far out, and joyless."

While they were in Los Angeles the Velvets did some more sessions at T.T.G. Studios in Hollywood, recording "I'm Waiting For The Man," "Venus In Furs," and "Heroin" with engineer Omi Haden. They also linked up with Tom Wilson, a gregarious African-American from Waco, Texas, who'd become a staff producer at Columbia Records, overseeing the recording of several groundbreaking albums by Bob Dylan (*The Times They Are a-Changin'*, *Another Side of Bob Dylan*, and *Bringing It All Back Home*) as well as the 1964 debut by Simon and Garfunkel. Wilson was in the process of moving from Columbia to head up the Verve Records division at MGM, and he promised the band a deal—if the musicians would be patient.

The wait dragged on through the rest of 1966 and into 1967: Adorned with the famous peelable banana cover art by Warhol, *The Velvet Underground & Nico* would only finally be released on March 12, 1967, a few months before *Sgt. Pepper's Lonely Hearts Club Band* signaled the start of the much-ballyhooed Summer of Love. In addition to the songs recorded at Scepter and T.T.G., the final album included one more tune, "Sunday Morning," recorded in November 1966 with Wilson in New York because he wanted the band to have "a commercial single." The original plan was to let Nico sing the track—she thought of the uncharacteristically upbeat tune as "Sun-day mourning"—but Reed insisted that he do it himself. Relations between the musicians and their chanteuse were already souring, and by the time the album arrived in record stores, the band and Warhol were going their separate ways as well.

Warhol's short attention span was infamous; the group wasn't returning much on his investment of time or money,

Nico, Lou Reed, and John Cale rehearse at the rented quarters in the Castle before the band's shows at the Trip in Hollywood, May 1966. *Lisa Law*

The Exploding Plastic Inevitable hits Los Angeles with Andy Warhol's films, light show, and dancers Mary Woronov and Gerard Malanga. *Lisa Law*

and he seemed to be siding with Nico as her star rose after her role in his film *Chelsea Girls* (which featured contributions from Reed and Cale on the soundtrack). "The final nail in the coffin of Lou Reed's collaborative relationship with Andy Warhol came at the end of May 1967, when Warhol took an entourage to the Cannes Film Festival in France to show *Chelsea Girls*—excluding the Velvets," Bockris wrote in *Transformer: The Lou Reed Story*. But Warhol already had performed his biggest service for the band.

"He just made it possible for us to be ourselves and go right ahead with it because he was Andy Warhol," Reed told *Musician* magazine in 1989. "In a sense, he really did produce [the first album], because he was this umbrella that absorbed all the attacks when we weren't large enough to be attacked . . . and as a consequence of him being the producer, we'd just walk in and set up and do what we always did and no one would stop it because Andy was the producer. Of course he didn't know anything about record production—but he didn't have to. He just sat there and said, 'Oooh, that's fantastic,' and the engineer would say, 'Oh, yeah! Right! It *is* fantastic, isn't it?'"

Reaction from reviewers was less enthusiastic, though by no means was it universally negative, as is sometimes contended today. "All in all, for what it is trying to express, this is a good album—not for those who desire to hear the usual popular music, but for those who desire to hear a very unusual, perhaps even experimental type of music," Timothy Jacobs wrote in the underground journal *Vibrations*. The record's commercial performance was underwhelming—it debuted on the *Billboard* Top 200 Albums Chart at 199, peaked at 171 on December 16, 1967, and dropped off at 193 on January 6, 1968—but it was victim as much of the delay in its release and a series of marketing problems (including a lawsuit filed by Factory dancer Eric Emerson for unauthorized use of his photo on the back cover) as it was the lack of popular acceptance.

The ideas that the Velvets were alone in spreading bad vibes during the sunny heyday of hippy and that they had nothing in common with psychedelia also are untrue. The Thirteenth Floor Elevators, the Byrds of "Eight Miles High," and many of the psychedelic garage bands that Lenny Kaye compiled on the *Nuggets* album all conjured similar free-form bum-trip excursions in rock during the same period, and while the Velvets undeniably preferred

nevertheless persisted that Warhol's banana was laced with LSD. In many ways the Exploding Plastic Inevitable was similar to the sensory assaults Pink Floyd was delivering in London and Ken Kesey's acid tests were providing in San Francisco. In New York, grungy folkies the Fugs and the Holy Modal Rounders were addressing similar taboo lyrical concerns, while the Beatles also dabbled in the power of drone with "Tomorrow Never Knows" on *Revolver* in 1966. The Velvets were not totally unique in anything they did; they simply were more extreme and uncompromising.

Listening to *The Velvet Underground & Nico* today, when the shock of the new has long since faded, the most striking things about the album are the enduring artistry of the songwriting and the musician-ship and the fact that it contains the seeds of everything the group would explore for the rest of its career. The Velvets would extend the chaotic experimentation of "The Black Angel's Death Song" and "European Son" even further with *White Light/White Heat*; they would go beyond "I'll Be Your Mirror" and "Femme Fatale" to dig even deeper into their quiet, intro-spective souls with the self-titled third album, and they would up the ante on pop songs such as "Sunday Morning" (which recalled the Beach Boys circa *Pet Sounds*) and the gleefully misogynistic "There She Goes Again" (a blatant rewrite of Marvin Gaye's "Hitchhike") with the more straightfor-ward rock 'n' roll of *Loaded*. But all in good time . . . 🕶

May 28, 1966

"Out of sight" ...Sonny Bono, actor.

"It's like eating a banana nut Brillo Pad" ... David Crosby, Byrd.

"It doesn't leave anything for the imagination" ... Tony Hicks, Holly.

A Happening!

What is it? It's Andy Warhol, it's The Plastic Inevitable, it's The Velvet Underground, it's Nico, it's a pair of dancers, a candle, two whips, a candy bar, a violin, a pop bottle and movies.

It's from New York and it's on the West Coast for the first time at The Trip in Hollywood. It's going to other parts of the nation soon.

It's drawing crowds of curious celebrities and it's confusing crowds of curious.

It's happening.

See it for yourself, no questions allowed.

BEAT Photos: Howard L. Bingham

"I'm glad I've got short hair" ... Ryan O'Neal, Rodney

"The Velvet Underground should go back underground and practice" ... Barry McGuire, chicken rancher.

"It's where entertaining's going" ... John Phillips, Papa.

The Beat newspaper chronicled the Exploding Plastic Inevitable show at the Trip with a photomontage showing a stunned-looking crowd.

Poster and handbills, Exploding Plastic Inevitable, Fillmore West Auditorium, San Francisco, California, May 27, 1966. The band's run at the Fillmore was extended through May 29.
Artist: Wes Wilson

TICKET OUTLETS:
San Francisco
City Lights Books; Psychedelic Shop
Bally Lo - Union Square
S.F. State College, Hut T-1

Berkeley
Campus Records
Discount Records
A.S.U.C. Box Office

Sausalito
Rexall Pharmacy

Menlo Park
Kepler's Books

Santa Rosa

Apex Book Store

Poster, Exploding Plastic Inevitable, Poor Richard's, Chicago, Illinois, June 21–26, 1966. The show was held over through July 3—even though Lou Reed missed this gig (he was recuperating from hepatitis at Beth Israel Hospital in New York) and Nico never showed because she was on holiday in Ibiza.

The Velvet Underground's first single—"All Tomorrow's Parties"/"I'll Be Your Mirror"—was released in July of 1966, preceding the LP.

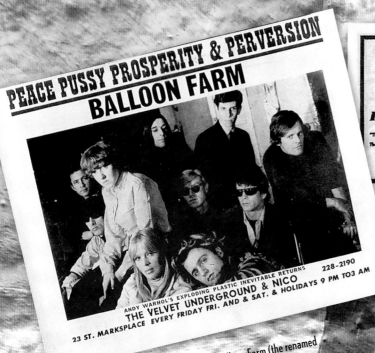

ANDY WARHOL'S EXPLODING PLASTIC INEVITABLE RETURNS   228-2190
THE VELVET UNDERGROUND & NICO
23 ST. MARKSPLACE EVERY FRIDAY FRI. AND & SAT. & HOLIDAYS 9 PM TO3 AM

Advertisements, Exploding Plastic Inevitable, Balloon Farm (the renamed Dom), New York City, October 1966.

ANDY WARHOL'S PLASTIC INEVITABLE
THE VELVET UNDERGROUND
Last New York Weekend **& NICO** *Last New York Weekend*

"The sound is a savage sense of atonal thrusts and electronic feedback. The lyrics combine sado-masoch istic frenzy with free association imagery. The whole sound seems to be the product of a secret marriage between Bob Dylan & Marquis de Sade." Richard Goldstein, N.Y. World Journal Tribune, Oct. 16, 1966

MUSIC-MOVIES-DANCE-LIGHTS-SLIDES-FREE FOOD -DRINK
BALLOON FARM 23 ST. MARKS PLACE FRI. & SAT. ONLY   228-2190

ANDY WARHOL'S
**EXPLODING PLASTIC
INEVITABLE RETURNS**
TO 23 ST. MARK'S PLACE

*The Velvet
Underground
& Nico*

Fri. & Sat. Only
BALLOON FARM
Tel. OR 4-2585

Last Chance To Dance At Andy Warhol's Disco-Flick
ANDY WARHOL'S NEW DISCO-FLICKA-THEQUE
THE EXPLODING PLASTIC INEVITABLE
live
ANDY WARHOL
THE VELVET UNDERGROUND AND NICO
SUPERSTARS GERARD MALANGA AND MARY WORONOV ON FILM ON STAGE ON VINYL
LIVE MUSIC, DANCING, ULTRA, SOUNDS, VISIONS, KINETIC LIGHTWORKS BY DANIEL WILLIAMS, FACES, HARLOT, HEDY, COUCH, BANANA, ETC., ETC. ALL IN THE SAME PLACE AT THE SAME TIME. "APOTHEOSIS OF POP" V.V.
MOVIES INCLUDING: VINYL, SLEEP, EAT, KISS, EMPIRE, WHIPS, FACES, HARLOT, HEDY, COUCH, BANANA, ETC., ETC. ALL IN THE SAME PLACE AT THE SAME TIME. "APOTHEOSIS OF POP" V.V.
"NEW POP SCENE" — N.Y. TIMES. "TOTAL MOLECULAR CORRUPTION" LESTER PERSKY
AT THE OPEN STAGE   23 ST. MARK'S PLACE (BET. 2nd & 3rd AVES.) 9-2 LAST PERFORMANCE SAT. APRIL 30
674-9742

SUNDAY OCT. 30
3 P.M. & 8:30 P.M.
ANDY WARHOL
Presents
HALLOWEEN
MOD
HAPPENING
THE EXPLODING
PLASTIC INEVITABLE
LEICESTER AIRPORT
Off Route 56, Leicester, Mass.

Poster, Exploding Plastic Inevitable, Leicester Airport, Leicester, Massachusetts, October 30, 1966.

ANDY WARHOL'S PLASTIC INEVITABLE

THE VELVET UNDERGROUND & NICO

MUSIC – MOVIES – DANCE – LIGHTS – SLIDES – FOOD – DRINK

23 ST. MARKS PLACE   FRI. & SAT. ONLY

BALLOON FARM   228-2190

IT'S ANDY WARHOL'S EXPLOSION!

EXPLODING PLASTIC INEVITABLE

IT'S THE CRASHING SOUND OF THE
VELVET UNDERGROUND "NICO"

IT'S UNDERGROUND MOVIES

IT'S STROBE LIGHTNING & MIRROR BALLS

IT'S WHERE ENTERTAINMENTS GOING

IT'S THE . . .   ★ ★ ★

CHRYSLER ART MUSEUM

PROVINCETOWN, MASS.

★   WED. thru SUN.   ★

AUG. 31 TO SEPT. 4

2 SHOWS 9 & 10:30 – FRI. at 12:00 ALSO

Metropolitan Show Print · 97 West Dedham St., Boston, Mass.

Posters, Exploding Plastic Inevitable, Chrysler Art Museum, Provincetown,
Massachusetts, August 31–September 4, 1966.

Nico plays piano in the spotlight at Toronto. *Ian MacEachern*

Sterling Morrison jams in front of one of Andy Warhol's projected films. *Ian MacEachern*

John Cale bows his electrified viola, strung with steel guitar strings. *Ian MacEachern*

Lit by the Exploding Plastic Inevitable's own strobe, Gerard Malanga cracks his whip to "Femme Fatale." *Ian MacEachern*

Lou Reed began using a hot-rodded Gretsch Country Gentleman guitar. Reed fitted the Gretsch with preamps and speed/tremolo controls to produce a chorus of notes behind every one he played. He added a Fender Stratocaster single-coil pickup for a more trebly tone. Reed also converted the Gretsch to stereo so he could get low bass and high treble simultaneously on different channels. *Ian MacEachern*

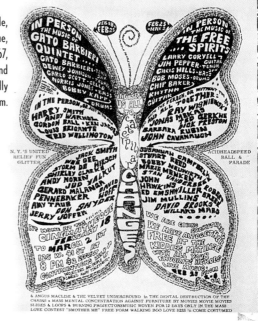

Poster, Exploding Plastic Inevitable, Film-Makers' Cinemathèque, New York City, February 18, 1967, featuring the Velvet Underground (as well as Angus MacLise) literally in the small print at the bottom.

A second single—"Sunday Morning"/"Femme Fatale"—was released in December 1966.

Poster, Exploding Plastic Inevitable, Carnaby Street Fun Festival, Michigan State Fairgrounds, Detroit, Michigan, November 20, 1966.

Poster, "The Steve Paul & Andy Warhol Underground Amateur Hour," Steve Paul's Scene, New York City, January 2–14, 1967. *Collection of The Andy Warhol Museum, Pittsburgh; Founding Collection, Contribution The Andy Warhol Foundation for the Visual Arts, Inc.*

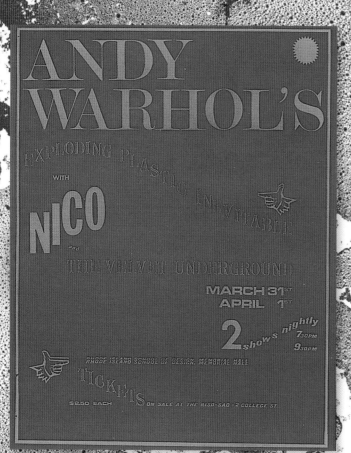

ANDY WARHOL'S
EXPLODING PLASTIC INEVITABLE
WITH
NICO
AND
THE VELVET UNDERGROUND

MARCH 31ST
APRIL 1ST

2 shows nightly 7:30PM
9:30PM

RHODE ISLAND SCHOOL OF DESIGN, MEMORIAL HALL

TICKETS
$2.50 EACH ON SALE AT THE RISD-SAO - 2 COLLEGE ST

The Velvet Underground lit by Warhol's colored slides at the Rhode Island School of Design shows. *Bill Carner*

John Cale in action at the Rhode Island School of Design. *Bill Carner*

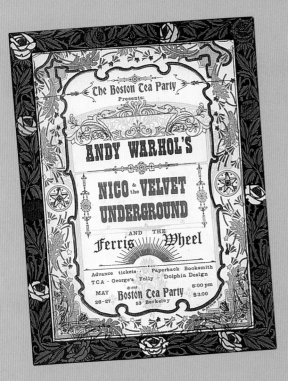

Advertisement, Exploding Plastic Inevitable, the Gymnasium, New York City, April 30, 1967.

Handbills, Exploding Plastic Inevitable, Boston Tea Party, Boston, Massachusetts, May 26–27, 1967. This marked the final show with Nico. *Artist: D. Arthur Hahn & Dolphin Design*

A NEW HAPPENING DISCOTHEQUE
JOINS THE SWINGING SIDE OF SINGLE NEW YORK

THE GYMNASIUM

with
ANDY WARHOL
presenting
NICO
and the
VELVET UNDERGROUND

And don't miss
IN NEW YORK MAGAZINE'S

NATIONAL SWINGER'S NITE

SUNDAY, APRIL 30, at 6 P.M.

with ANDY, NICO, LIVE BAND
and FREAK OUT LIGHTS
making the wildest swing-in
the EAST SIDE'S ever seen.

424 E. 71st ST. (between York & 1st)
(SOKOL HALL)

ADMISSION $2*
777-2210
Specially reduced for this nite only

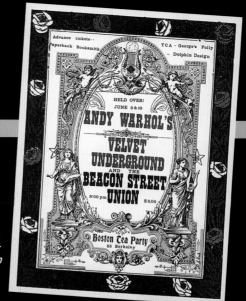

Handbill, Boston Tea Party, Boston, Massachusetts, June 9–10, 1967.
Artist: D. Arthur Hahn

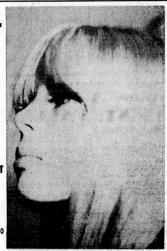

ANDY WARHOL
PRESENTS
Nico
SINGING TO THE SOUNDS OF
The Velvet
Underground
AT THE UNDERGROUND BAR AT
THE NEW
MOD-DOM

23 ST. MARK'S PLACE   777-2210
APPEARING NITELY EXCEPT SUN. & MON.

Opening Thursday, December 19th
COCKTAIL HOUR
5 to 8 p.m.

The Blue Angel Lounge
featuring the intimate songs of
Nico

All drinks 85¢   No minimum; no cover
152 East 55th Street   PLaza 3-5998

After leaving the Velvet Underground, Nico performed as a solo artist at the New Dom and other New York City venues. At first, she sang along to a tape-recorded rhythm track; later she was backed at various times by Sterling Morrison, Tim Hardin, and Jackson Browne.

NICO. You've seen her in Andy Warhol's Exploding Plastic Underground . . . starring in his "Chelsea Girls." They call her the Dietrich of the velvet underground. Nonsense. She's Nico. And you can hear her making the scene on Verve as **NICO: CHELSEA GIRL.**
V/V6-5032
The Sound of the Now Generation is on
Verve Records is a division of Metro-Goldwyn-Mayer Inc.

Advertisement for Nico's debut solo album, *Chelsea Girl*, 1967. Produced by Tom Wilson, the LP included five tracks written by Velvet Underground members.

Poster, "Tune In, Turn on Murray the K, WOR-FM," 1967. *Collection of The Andy Warhol Museum, Pittsburgh; Founding Collection, Contribution The Andy Warhol Foundation for the Visual Arts, Inc.*

The Velvet Underground takes the stage at the Trauma. *Billy Name/ Ovoworks/Time Life Pictures/Getty Images*

Poster, the Trauma, Philadelphia, Pennsylvania, July 19–22 and 26–29, 1967.
Artist: Karen Fritz

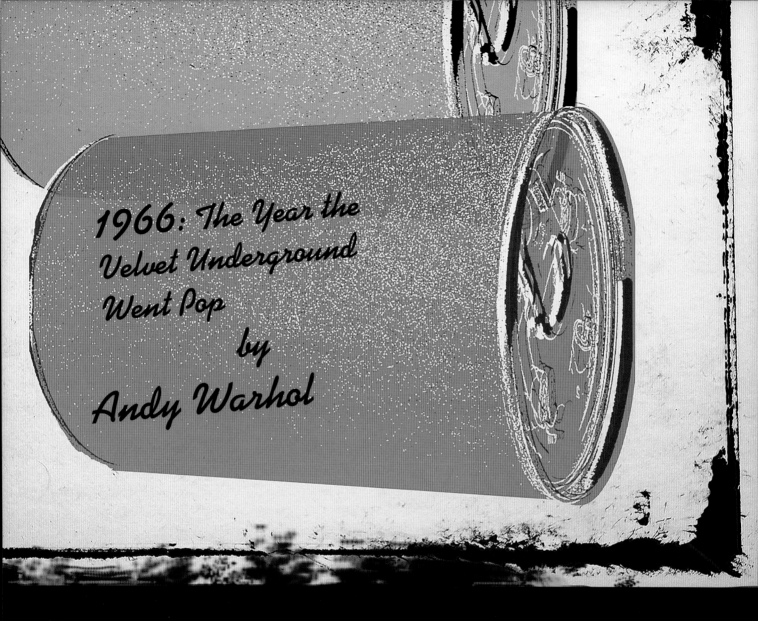

1966: The Year the Velvet Underground Went Pop

by Andy Warhol

For Andy Warhol and his followers at the Silver Factory, the highlight of 1966 was the adoption of the Velvet Underground as their very own rock 'n' roll band. In Warhol's memoir, POPism: The Warhol Sixties, he describes with an amphetamine rush of enthusiasm his meeting the VU and their first performances with the grand spectacle that would become the Exploding Plastic Inevitable. And he describes the Velvets' scene with much the same detail as Lou Reed would later chronicle it in his post-VU song, "Walk On The Wild Side." For Warhol, 1966 was the year the Velvets went pop.

A s '65 turned to '66, the big new interest at the Factory was a group of musicians that called themselves the Velvet Underground. For New Year's, the Velvets, Edie [Sedgwick], Paul [Morrissey], Gerard [Malanga], and I all went to the Apollo Theater up in Harlem, then raced back downtown to watch ourselves on the evening news. Eventually we passed out in front of the TV. Then later, when I went out on the street to go home, it was impossible to get a cab because the great Transit Strike had started that midnight, just as John Lindsay, the city's Hollywood-handsome, love-comic beautiful new mayor, was stepping into office. That was another "happening," sort of like the blackout—people walking hundreds of blocks to work or riding bikes or hitching rides.

In January, Jonas [Mekas] moved the Film-Makers' Cinemathèque from Lafayette to West 41st Street. He was in the middle of a series called Expanded Cinema where artists like Jack Smith and La Monte Young and Robert Whitman would combine cinema images and projectors with live action and music. I remember Oldenburg's piece where he dragged a bicycle down the aisle from the last row of the theater while a movie was being projected, and I remember Rauschenberg where he was a walking light metaphor, so beautiful to look at, electrified and standing on glass bricks holding a live wire and fluorescent tubes—the artist Arman had made glass shoes for him so that the electricity wouldn't be conducted.

We'd met the Velvets through a filmmaker friend of Jonas's named Barbara Rubin, who was one of the first people to get multimedia interest going around New York. She knew a lot of rock and folk performers, and she'd sometimes bring people like Donovan and the Byrds by the Factory.

The Velvets had done tapes for filmmakers to use while they projected their movies and they'd played live behind the screen during some screenings at the Lafayette Street Cinemathèque. But where we first really became aware of how fabulous and

[continued on 84]

Andy Warhol with "his" rock 'n' roll band, Hollywood Hills, 1966. *Gerard Malanga*

Andy Warhol at work in 1966 in the Silver Factory on the banana images that became the Velvet Underground's logo. *Hervé Gloaguen/Rapho/Eyedea*

[continued from 81

demented their act was at the Cafe Bizarre on West 3rd Street—"On Go-Go Street for nine bucks a night," as Lou Reed, the sort of lead Velvet, put it.

When Barbara Rubin asked Gerard to help her make a movie of the Velvets playing at the Bizarre, Gerard asked Paul Morrissey to help, and Paul said why didn't I come along, and so we all went down there to see them. The Bizarre management wasn't too thrilled with them. Their music was beyond the pale—way too loud and insane for any tourist coffeehouse clientele. People would leave looking dazed and damaged. Anyway, the Velvets were about to get fired. We talked to them a little bit that same night while Barbara and her crew went through the audience pushing the blinding sun gun lights and the cameras in people's faces and asking, "Are you uptight? Are you uptight?" until they reacted, and then she would hold the cameras and lights on them while they got madder or cringed more or ran away or whatever.

We liked the Velvets and invited them to come by the Factory.

Paul wanted to do some shows with them. Coincidentally, we'd just been approached by a producer who'd taken over a film studio out on Long Island that he wanted to turn into a discotheque. He claimed that this studio was originally the airplane hangar that Lindbergh took off from. It was around seventeen thousand square feet and had a three-thousand-person capacity and he was going to call it Murray the K's World. He said he wanted the Factory crew to be disco mascots and hang out there every night making movies so he could get publicity for the place. Paul thought there should be a house band since Jordan Christopher's house band at Arthur did so well, and the producer said that if we could come up with a band, maybe he'd just call the place Andy Warhol's World.

So when we'd gone to the Bizarre to see the Velvets that time, what Paul was trying to do was psyche out how they'd be in a big airplane hangar of a discotheque and how they'd go down with the kids. If any band then could fill up seventeen thousand square feet with blasting sound, it was the Velvets. We liked the idea that their drummer was a girl, that was unusual. Sterling Morrison and Lou Reed—and even Maureen Tucker—wore jeans and T-shirts, but John Cale, the Welsh electric viola player, had a more parochial look—white shirts and black pants and rhinestone jewelry (a dog collar–type necklace and bracelet) and long black spiky hair and some kind of English accent. And Lou looked good and pubescent then—Paul thought the kids out on the Island would identify with that.

Another idea we had in mind when we went to check out the Velvets was that they might be a good band to play behind Nico, an incredible German beauty who'd just arrived in New York from London. She looked like she could have made the trip over right at the front of a Viking ship, she had that kind of face and body. Although Nico got more and more into the swirling capes and medieval monastery look as the sixties went on, when she first came on the scene she dressed very mod and spiffy in white wool pants, double-breasted blazers, beige cashmere turtlenecks, and those pilgrim-looking shoes with the big buckles on them. She had straight shoulder-length blond hair with bangs, blue eyes, full lips, wide cheekbones—the works. And she had this very strange way of speaking. People described her voice as everything from eery, to bland and smooth, to slow and hollow, to a "wind in a drainpipe," to an "IBM computer with a Garbo accent." She sounded the same strange way when she sang, too.

Gerard had met her in London that spring and given her the Factory number to call if she ever came to New York. She called us from a Mexican restaurant and we went right over to meet her. She was sitting at a table with a pitcher in front of her, dipping her long beautiful fingers into the sangria, lifting out slices of wine-soaked oranges. When she saw us, she tilted her head to the side and brushed her hair back with her other hand and said very slowly, "I only like the fooood that flooooats in the wiiine."

During dinner, Nico told us that she'd been on TV in England in a rock show called "Ready, Steady, Go!" and right there she pulled a demo 45 rpm out of her bag of a song called "I'll Keep It With Mine" that had been written for her, she said, by Bob Dylan, who'd been over there touring. (It was one of a few pressings that had Dylan playing the piano on it, and eventually Judy Collins recorded it.) Nico said that Al Grossman had heard it and told her that if she came to the United States, he'd manage her. When she said that, it didn't sound too promising, because we'd heard Edie telling us so much that she was "under contract" to Grossman and nothing much seemed to be happening for her—having a well-known manager was never a guarantee that things would really happen for you. (We were still seeing Edie, but we weren't showing her films anymore—the idea of the Edie Sedgwick Retrospective at the Cinemathèque had fizzled out, and it looked like our contribution to the Expanded Cinema series would be something with the Velvet Underground instead.)

Nico had cut a record called "I'm Not Sayin'" in London (Andrew Oldham, the Stones' producer, had produced it), and she'd also been in *La Dolce Vita*. She had a young son—we'd heard rumors that the father was Alain Delon and Paul asked her about that immediately because Delon was one of his favorite

Black on white: the Velvet Underground plays at the Paraphernalia Store in New York City in March 1966. *Charlie Gillett Archive/Redferns and Nat Finkelstein*

actors, and Nico said yes, that it was true and that the boy was in Europe with Alain's mother. The minute we left the restaurant Paul said that we should use Nico in the movies and find a rock group to play for her. He was raving that she was "the most beautiful creature that ever lived."

Nico was a new type of female superstar. Baby Jane and Edie were both outgoing, American, social, bright, excited, chatty—whereas Nico was weird and untalkative. You'd ask her something and she'd maybe answer you five minutes later. When people described her, they used words like memento mori and macabre. She wasn't the type to get up on a table and dance, the way Edie or Jane might; in fact, she'd rather hide under the table than dance on top of it. She was mysterious and European, a real moon goddess type.

I was invited to speak at the annual banquet of the New York Society for Clinical Psychiatry by the doctor who was chairman of the event. I told him I'd be glad to "speak," if I could do it through movies, that I'd show *Harlot* and *Henry Geldzahler*, and he said fine. Then when I met the Velvets I decided that I wanted to "speak" with them instead, and he said fine to that, too.

So one evening in the middle of January everybody at the Factory went over to the Delmonico Hotel where the banquet was taking place. We got there just as it was starting. There were about three hundred psychiatrists and their mates and dates—and all they'd been told was that they were going to see movies after dinner. The second the main course was served, the Velvets started to blast and Nico started to wail. Gerard and Edie jumped up on the stage and started dancing, and the doors flew open and Jonas Mekas and Barbara Rubin with her crew of people with cameras and bright lights came storming into the room and rushing over to all the psychiatrists asking them things like:

"What does her vagina feel like?"
"Is his penis big enough?"
"Do you eat her out? Why are you getting embarrassed? You're a psychiatrist; you're not supposed to get embarrassed!"

Edie had come with Bobby Neuwirth. While the crews filmed and Nico sang her Dylan song, Gerard noticed (he told me this later) that Edie was trying to sing, too, but that even in the incredible din, it was obvious she didn't have a voice. He always looked back on that night as the last time she ever went out with us in public, except for a party here and there. He thought that she'd felt upstaged that night, that she'd realized Nico was the new girl in town. .

Nico and Edie were so different, there was no good reason to compare them, really. Nico was so cool, and Edie was so bubbly. But the sad thing was, Edie was taking a lot of heavy drugs, and she was getting vaguer and vaguer. Her Society lady attitude toward pills had changed to an addict attitude. Some of her good friends tried to help her, but she wouldn't listen to them. She said she wanted a "career" and that she'd get one since Grossman was managing her. But how can you have a career when you don't have the discipline to work at anything?

Gerard had noticed how lost Edie looked at that psychiatrists' banquet, but I can't really say that I noticed; I was too fascinated watching the psychiatrists. They really were upset, and some of them started to leave, the ladies in their long dresses and the men in their black ties. As if the music—the feedback, actually—that the Velvets were playing wasn't enough to drive them out, the movie lights were blinding them and the questions were making them turn red and stutter because the kids wouldn't let up, they just kept on asking more. And Gerard did his notorious Whip Dance. I loved it all.

The next day there were long write-ups about the banquet in both the *Tribune* and the *Times*: "SHOCK TREATMENT FOR PSYCHIATRISTS" and "SYNDROMES POP AT DELMONICO'S." It couldn't have happened to a better group of people.

In January, when the Cinemathèque moved to 41st Street, the Velvets and Nico played together again and we screened *Vinyl* and *Empire* and *Eat* in the background and Barbara Rubin and her crew ran around the audience as usual with movie cameras and bright lights. Gerard was up on the stage whipping a long strip of phosphorescent tape in the air. The whole event was called "Andy Warhol Up Tight."

These were still the days when you could live on practically no money, and that was about what the Velvets seemed to have. Lou told me that for weeks at a time he and John would go without eating anything but oatmeal and that for money they'd donate blood or pose for the weekly tabloids that needed photos to illustrate their shock stories. The caption to one of Lou's pictures said he was a maniac sex killer who'd murdered fourteen children and recorded their screams so that he could jerk off to the tape every midnight in a Kansas barn; and John's picture appeared with the story of a man who'd killed his lover because the lover was going to marry his sister and the man didn't want his sister to marry a fag.

Paul asked Lou how the Velvets happened to have a girl drummer and he said, "Very simple. Sterling knew her brother, who had an amplifier, and he told us we could use it if we let his sister drum for us." They needed more amplifiers, though, and we called up a few equipment places trying to get them free, but the best we could do was get a few dollars knocked off when we paid cash. Then the Velvets started practicing at the Factory with their drums, tambourine, harmonica, guitars, Autoharp, maracas, kazoo, car horn, and pieces of glass that they hit.

A reporter once asked Paul if we paid the Velvets, and when Paul said no, the reporter wanted to know what they lived on. Paul had to consider that for a second, then he offered, "Well, they eat a lot at parties." . . .

The early lineup of the Exploding Plastic Inevitable poses in the Silver Factory. Clockwise from left: Andy Warhol, Sterling Morrison, Moe Tucker, John Cale, Lou Reed, and dancers Mary Woronov and Gerard Malanga. *Nat Finkelstein*

All during January and February we were meeting with the disco producer about opening the airplane hangar discotheque with the Erupting (it wasn't "Exploding" yet) Plastic Inevitable (E.P.I.) in Roosevelt Field in April. The producer had come down to the Expanded Cinema series at the Cinemathèque the night the Velvets played there. It was the first time he'd ever heard them perform, and although he'd said "great, great" when we asked him how he liked the show, looking back on it, I can see that he must have hated it but didn't want to cancel with us till he covered himself by finding something to take our place.

In March we drove down to Rutgers to play at their college film society—Paul, Gerard, Nico, Ingrid Superstar, a photographer named Nat Finklestein, a blond girl named Susanna, Barbara Rubin, a young kid named Danny Williams who was working the lights, and an Englishman named John Wilcock, who was one of the first journalists to cover the counterculture. We went into the Rutgers cafeteria to eat before the show, and the students couldn't take their eyes off Nico, she was so beautiful it was unreal, or off Susanna, who was going around picking food off their plates and dropping it grape-style into her mouth. Barbara Rubin was filming the kids, and the guards were following her telling her to stop, then somebody came over wanting to check our "cafeteria pass" and Gerard started yelling at them and there was a big commotion. We got kicked out, of course, but fortunately it all made people want to see the show, which until then hadn't been doing too well in advance sales.

We did two shows for over 650 people. We screened *Vinyl* and *Lupe* and also movies of Nico and the Velvets while they were playing. It was fantastic to see Nico singing with a big movie of her face right behind her. Gerard was dancing with two long shining flashlights, one in each hand, twirling them like batons. The audience was mesmerized—when a college kid set off the fire alarm system by holding a match near it, nobody paid any attention to it.

I was behind one of the projectors, moving the images around. The kids were having a lot of trouble dancing, because the songs sometimes started out with a beat but then the Velvets would get too frenetic and burn themselves out, losing the audience long before that. They were like audio-sadists, watching the dancers trying to cope with the music.

A few days later, we left New York for Ann Arbor in a rented van to play at the University of Michigan. Nico drove, and that was an experience. I still don't know if she had a license. She'd only been in this country a little while and she'd keep forgetting and drive on the British side of the road. And the van was a real problem—whenever it stopped, it was hard to get it started again, and not one of us knew anything about cars.

A cop stopped us at a hamburger drive-in near Toledo when a waitress got upset and complained to him because we kept changing orders, and when he asked, "Who's in charge here?" Lou shoved me forward and told him, "Of all people—Drella!" ("Drella" was a nickname somebody had given me that stuck more than I wanted it to. Ondine and a character named Dorothy Dyke used it all the time—they said it came from combining Dracula and Cinderella.) We spent the night in a motel near there, and once again it was the-boys-in-one-room-the-girls-in-the-other scene, even though somebody kept telling the little old lady who ran the place, "But we're all queer."

At Ann Arbor, we met up with Danny Fields, who'd just been made the editor of a teenage magazine, *Datebook*. He was out there covering the concert. I hadn't seen him in a while.

"Well," he laughed, "I finally have an identity of my own. Up until now, I was just a groupie with no real reason to exist."

"And to think you launched your career," Lou reminded him, "getting out the wrong side of a limousine."

Nico's driving really was insane when we hit Ann Arbor. She was shooting across sidewalks and over people's lawns. We finally pulled up in front of a nice big comfortable-looking house, and everyone started unloading the van. Danny wouldn't believe that anyone was going to let "a truckload of freaks" pull up and walk right into their house until a beautiful woman came running out to meet us. She was Ann Wehrer, whose husband, Joseph, was involved with the early "happenings" and had arranged for the E.P.I. to come out there.

Ann Arbor went crazy. At last the Velvets were a smash. I'd sit on the steps in the lobby during intermissions and people from the local papers and school papers would interview me, ask about my movies, what we were trying to do. "If they can take it for ten minutes, then we play it for fifteen," I'd explain. "That's our policy. Always leave them wanting less."

Danny remembers that one interviewer asked if my movies had been influenced by the thirties and forties and that I told him, "No, the tens. Thomas Edison really influenced me." And as a matter of fact, we had a strobe light with us for the first time. The guy we rented spotlights from in New York had brought it to the Factory to show us—none of us had ever seen one before. They weren't being used yet in the clubs. The strobes were magical, they went perfectly with the chaos music the

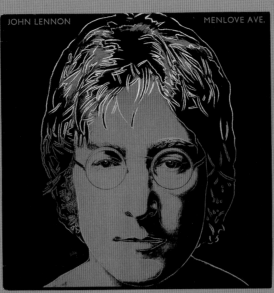

The "Banana Album" was not Andy Warhol's first—or, only—album cover. Warhol was a prolific artist and designer of covers, beginning in 1949. He created art and concepts for albums of music from classical to folk; rock 'n' roll was a late arrival on the scene. Along with *The Velvet Underground & Nico*, Warhol designed the cover for *White Light/White Heat* for the band. After the iconic banana image, Warhol's other most famous LP cover was also an unabashed case of phallic worship: the Rolling Stones' 1971 *Sticky Fingers*.

Velvets played, and that long piece of phosphorescent green Sylvania tape that Gerard was now using for his dance numbers, whipping that around, looked terrific when the strobes flashed on it.

When we got back to New York, Paul tried to pin the disco producer down to a definite date for the opening, but he just kept assuring us, "Don't worry." Then somehow we found out that he'd already hired the Young Rascals to open the place.

Paul and I went down to meet the Velvets at the Café Figaro—they were staying at an apartment just down the street—to tell them that the big gig had fallen through. When we walked in, they were already there, sitting around in their wraparound "girl watcher" dark glasses, all in a great mood, full of plans for the gala opening.

"We have a new number using John's thunder machine," Lou said as we sat down; then he laughed. "For the second time this week, a cop threatened us. He came up to the apartment and told us to go out into the country someplace if we were going to play that kind of stuff. This is a week after he stopped us on our way out the door and accused us of throwing human shit out our windows. . . . The awful thing is that it was just possible." Lou's voice was dry and flat, and he had droll timing with a little Jack Benny in it.

"We want to play all in the dark so the music will be the only thing. Tomorrow we're going to go to used car lots and buy hundreds of car horns and wire them all up so the honking will be nonstop."

"Yes, no, that's great, but listen—" Paul started to tell them, but Lou just went on, more and more enthusiastic.

"We're going to play some of the ferocious songs that no one listens to anymore—the ones that run underneath everything we usually play—like 'Smoke from Your Cigarette' and 'I Need a Sunday Kind of Love' and 'Later for You, Baby'—everybody's going crazy over all the old blues people, but let's not forget about the Spaniels and people like that. And we're working on Sterl to play trumpet again; he's been too busy looking for a psychiatrist to get him out of the army." Sterling was right across the table, telling John about a friend of his with aquaphobia who slept on air mattresses in the Hamptons in case the sea level rose and carried rubber diver's fins in the backseat of his car in case the 59th Street Bridge should ever collapse while he was crossing it. "He feels that with the fins, he won't be screwed. . . ." Sterling was an on-again off-again English lit student but he struck you as a preoccupied scientist type. His

thought patterns seemed very methodical. It was as if he got up in the morning, got a certain thought, then spent all day developing it—he might, say, pause for an hour, but when he started talking again, it would be to make an "additional point," or to "clarify," no matter what everyone else had been talking about in between.

I noticed that Paul was eavesdropping on the conversation of two people at the next table. Incredibly, they were talking about a big Polish dance hall they'd just rented over on St. Mark's Place that they didn't know what to do with. Paul swiveled around and introduced himself. He told them he lived around that neighborhood and hadn't ever noticed a big dance hall. The two introduced themselves—they were Jackie Cassen and Rudy Stern. They told us they did "sculpture with light" and that they'd rented this big Polish dance hall called Stanley's the Dom (Polsky Dom Narodny—Dom is Polish for "home") but that they wouldn't be ready to use it till May and that they didn't know what to do with it for April. Paul asked if we could go and see it right away. We left the Velvets at the Figaro without telling them about the airplane hangar falling through—it's always better to wait with bad news till you have some good news to go with it.

The Dom was perfect, just what we wanted—it had to be the biggest discotheque dance floor in Manhattan, and there was a balcony, too. We sublet it immediately from Jackie and Rudy—I gave them the rent check, Paul had a fight with the owner over the insurance, then we signed a few papers, and the very next day we were down there painting the place white so we could project movies and slides on the walls. We started dragging prop-type odds and ends over from the Factory—five movie projectors, five carousel-type projectors where the image changes every ten seconds and where, if you put two images together, they bounce. These colored things would go on top of the five movies, and sometimes we'd let the sound tracks come through. We also brought down one of those big revolving speakeasy mirrored balls—we had it lying around the Factory and we thought it would be great to bring those back. (The balls really caught on after we revived the look, and pretty soon they were standard fixtures in every discotheque you walked into.) We had a guy come down with more spotlights and strobes that we wanted to rent—we were going to shine them on the Velvets and all around the audience during the show. Of course, we had no idea if people would come all the way down to St. Mark's Place for night life. All the downtown action had always been in the West Village—the East Village was Babushkaville. But by renting the Dom ourselves, we didn't have

The Exploding Plastic Inevitable plays with light show, strobes, movies, and mirror reflecting ball at the Trauma, Philadelphia, Pennsylvania, 1967.
Billy Name/Ovoworks, Inc.

to worry about whether "management" liked us or not, we could just do whatever we wanted to. And the Velvets were thrilled—in the Dom, the "house band" finally found a house. They could even walk to work.

The Velvets were staying in an apartment on 3rd Street in the West Village above a firehouse, across the street from the Gold Bug, near a Carvel place and a drugstore. The apartment belonged to Tom O'Horgan, but Tom had sublet it to Stanley Amos, who was living in the back part (the front and back apartments were joined in the middle by a semisecret doorway), and all of Tom's furniture and fixtures were still in it. In the early days of the Velvet Underground, everybody from the Factory spent a lot of time just hanging around down there, going to Chinatown at two in the morning, then up to the Flick on Second Avenue in the Fifties for ice cream at four, or over to the Brasserie.

Tom's apartment looked just like a stage set. The living room was raised and there were long mirrors on both sides of the door with primitive instruments hanging down them from the ceiling. And there were lots of dried flowers and a big black coffin and a couple of chairs with lions' heads on the arms. The room itself was pretty bare—just a few big pieces of furniture. And then there was the heating system—a fifteen-foot gold dragon built onto the ceiling with flames from the heater shooting out its open mouth.

People on amphetamine didn't really have "apartments," they had "nests"—usually one or two rooms that held fourteen to forty people, with everyone paranoid that somebody would steal their stash or their only magenta Magic Marker or let the water in the bathtub overflow into the pharmacy downstairs. John Cale used to sit in the front room for days and days with his electric viola, barely moving. Maureen—Mo—the girl drummer, was somebody I could never figure out: she was very innocent and sweet and shy, so then what was she doing there?

The foyer of Stanley's apartment in the back was dark and had jungle murals of a stuffed parrot and of monkeys eating oranges painted on the walls. The only light came from a big black spider lamp whose tail lit up. Then you walked through another small hall into a library that had a fur rug and a beaded lamp and a brick wall, and into the main room, where there was a wonderful piece of art by Johnny Dodd—a portable wall of sixty-one thousand canceled George Washington postage stamp heads cut out with a nail clipper. (Johnny had put an ad in the

voice to get all the stamps.) There were Tiffany lamps all over the place, too, and Art Nouveau Mucha prints in colors like beige and dark green of women with flowing hair, and wind-up Indians beating tom-toms, and lots of tapestries and Persian rugs. It looked like a battle of the set decorators.

There was a houseboy who came in once every few days, and Stanley explained that this boy was a homosexual, a Roman Catholic, and an alcoholic who'd dress up in little sailor suits to go out cruising but first he always had to get drunk, otherwise he felt too guilty. He straightened up Stanley's apartment to make the extra money to get drunk on. It was a good thing Stanley had him, too—after the Glitter Festivals.

Stanley had a bureau drawer that was completely filled with bags of glitter—no clothes or anything, just glitter. He would open the drawer and pass out the bags, and about half the people there would drop acid and shower sparkles in the air till the whole house was covered in them and Judson dancers would twirl through the room with flowers in their hair and the whole floor would change color because it was the multicolored kind of glitter. . . .

The other half of the room would be paranoid on amphetamine, staring at the half that was tripping on the LSD. They were each other's audience.

Lou and Ondine would have furious fights over trading Desoxyn for Obetrols—Desoxyn was twice as expensive and had fifteen milligrams of Methedrine, whereas Obetrols apparently had that much Meth plus something like five milligrams of sulfate. I could never figure out what they were talking about, which one was better. . . .

We took out a half-page ad in that week's Voice that read:

Come Blow Your Mind

the Silver Dream Factory presents the first

ERUPTING PLASTIC INEVITABLE

WITH
Andy Warhol
The Velvet Underground
AND
Nico

THE VELVET UNDERGROUND   EXCLUSIVELY ON MGM/ VERVE RECORDS R-1494

Verve promotional photograph for the release of *The Velvet Underground & Nico. Collection of The Andy Warhol Museum, Pittsburgh; Museum Loan, Sterling Morrison Archives, Collection of Martha Morrison*

standing next to me one night on the Dom balcony that looked out over all the action, "paaaaarting."

All that month the limousines pulled up outside the Dom. Inside, the Velvets played so loud and crazy I couldn't even begin to guess the decibels, and there were images projected everywhere, one on top of the other. I'd usually watch from the balcony or take my turn at the projectors, slipping different-colored gelatin slides over the lenses and turning movies like *Harlot*, *The Shoplifter*, *Couch*, *Banana*, *Blow Job*, *Sleep*, *Empire*, *Kiss*, *Whips*, *Face*, *Camp*, *Eat* into all different colors. Stephen Shore and Little Joey and a Harvard kid named Danny Williams would take turns operating the spotlights while Gerard and Ronnie [Cutrone] and Ingrid and Mary Might (Woronov) danced sadomasochistic style with the whips and flashlights and the Velvets played and the different-colored hypnotic dot patterns swirled and bounced off the walls and the strobes flashed and you could close your eyes and hear cymbals and boots stomping and whips cracking and tambourines sounding like chains rattling. . . .

We put up the front money ourselves to produce the Velvets' first album, hoping that some record company would come along later and buy our tapes. We rented time for a couple of days in one of those small recording studios on Broadway, and it was just Paul and me in the control booth, and Little Joey, and Tom Wilson, who'd produced Bob Dylan and who happened to be a friend of ours, just there helping informally.

didn't have to worry—one of the things that was so great about them was they always sounded raw and crude.

Raw and crude was the way I liked our movies to look, and there's a similarity between the sound in that album and the texture of *Chelsea Girls*, which came out of the same time.

The Trip was a club on Sunset Strip that Donovan had told us about the last time he'd been up to the Factory, and right after that, a manager named Charlie Rothchild had mentioned to Paul that he could get a booking for the Velvets there from May 3 to 29. So Paul went out ahead of us to scout things and wound up renting the Castle from Jack Simmons, an actor with real estate savvy, for the Velvets to stay in. Back at the Factory, we packed up the whips and chains and strobes and mirrored ball and followed.

After the Velvets opened, a lot of people wondered if they could last the full three weeks, and critics wrote things like "The Velvet Underground should go back underground and practice." But the Velvets in their wraparound shades and tight striped pants went right on playing their demented New York music, even though the easygoing L.A. people just didn't appreciate it; some of them said it was the most destructive thing they'd ever heard. On opening night, a couple of the Byrds were in the audience, and Jim Morrison, who looked really intrigued, and Ryan O'Neal and Mama Cass were there, kicking up their heels. We read a great comment by Cher Bono the next day in one of the newspapers, and we picked it up for our ads—"It will replace nothing, except maybe suicide." But Sonny seemed to like it all—he stayed on after she left.

The Velvets had been playing the Trip less than a week when the sheriff's office closed it down—suddenly there was this sign on the door telling people to go see Johnny Rivers at the Whiskey A Go-Go down the street instead, which was owned by the same two guys who owned the Trip. It said in the papers that the estranged wife of one of the owners had filed suit for some money she claimed her husband owed her. We all got ready to leave town when somebody advised us that if we stayed in L.A. we would get paid for the whole run, but that if we left town, we'd forfeit it—there was some rule that the musicians' union can make them pay, so we stuck around and sent Local 47 out there after the money for us. (It took three years, but they collected it.) So we had till the end of May to sit it out in L.A.

The Velvets were at the Castle, and some of us were staying at the Tropicana Motel on Santa Monica Boulevard. The Castle was a big medieval stone structure in the Hollywood Hills—with dungeon rooms downstairs and beautiful grounds. It had views of Griffith Park and of all of L.A. and across the way you could see the Frank Lloyd Wright mansion that Bela Lugosi had lived in. Lots of rock groups had stayed at the Castle—Dylan had just been there—and lots more would be staying there all during the sixties. We were shuttling back and forth between the Castle and our motel. There didn't seem to be as much to do out there as in New York, so we were anxious to get home. Meanwhile, Bill Graham was calling us to come up to San

"I can't pay you much money, but I believe in the same beautiful things that you do," he said intensely, looking around at all of us.

Paul finally broke down and said okay, that we'd go there, but after Graham left, everyone dished the West Coast rhetoric—we weren't used to that kind of approach. "Was he serious?" Paul laughed. "Does he think we actually believe in this? What 'beautiful things'?"

That's what so many people never understood about us. They expected us to take the things we believed in seriously, which we never did—we weren't intellectuals.

Paul blamed LSD for the decline of humor in the sixties. He said the only person on LSD who had a sense of humor left was Timothy Leary.

In a way he was right, because when we went up to San Francisco, whenever we tried to have fun with somebody, they would act like "How dare you make a joke!" Everybody seemed to be taking the Cosmic Joke so seriously they didn't want you to make little uncosmic jokes. But on the other hand, the kids on acid did seem happy, enjoying all the simple things like hugs and kisses and nature.

The San Francisco scene was bands and audiences grooving together, sharing the experience, whereas the Velvets' style was to alienate people—they would actually play with their backs to the audience!

take." Graham didn't say anything, he just fumed. Paul knew he was driving him good and crazy so he kept it up. "You know, I think I'm really all for heroin, because if you take care of yourself it doesn't affect you physically." He took a tangerine out of his pocket and peeled it in one motion, letting the peels fall on the floor. "With heroin you never catch cold—it started in the United States as a cure for the common cold."

Paul was saying everything he could think of to offend Bill Graham's San Francisco sensibility, but in the end it was dropping the tangerine peels on the Fillmore floor—which he had done totally unconsciously—that brought on the showdown. Little things mean a lot. Graham stared down at the peels, and he got livid. I don't remember his exact words, but he started yelling—things like:

"You disgusting germs from New York! Here we are, trying to clean up everything, and you come out here with your disgusting minds and whips—!" Things along that line.

A few days later we all went up to Provincetown on Cape Cod where the Velvets were going to play at the Chrysler Museum. The silver lamé, leather people in our New York group looked totally alien to the tan, healthy-looking Massachusetts kids. When our people—Susan Bottomly, David, Gerard, Ronnie, Mary Might, Eric, Paul, Lou, John, Sterling, Maureen, Faison the road manager—sprawled out on the beach, they looked like a giant Clorox spot on the sand, all those pasty-white New York City bodies out there in a sea of summer tans. Gerard had on his leather bikini, and he looked confident that it would turn somebody on, but everybody up there seemed more into the Boston-Irish look.

Naturally the A-heads were going crazy because they were almost out of amphetamine, and they'd walk around the P-town streets with their hands cupped to their ears as if they were hard of hearing, going "A? A?" trying to score. The night the Velvets played, the police raided the show—somebody had tipped them off that the Velvets had stolen most of the leather braids and whips they were using in their act from a local handicrafts store that afternoon. When the police came in, Mary had just strapped Eric to a post and was doing the S & M whip-dance around him. They confiscated the whips and then undid Eric so they could confiscate the straps he was tied with.

The houses we'd rented got really disgusting in the couple of days we were there because the toilets all stopped up—it seemed like no matter where the Velvets went, the toilets would stop up—and so they started scooping handfuls of shit from the toilets and slinging it out the windows. I'd heard references to this habit of theirs, but you don't believe stories like that till you see people running by you with handfuls of dripping shit, laughing.

Edie Sedgwick and Gerard Malanga dance in the lights before the Velvet Underground. *Adam Ritchie/Redferns*

Peel Slowly and See
The Velvet Underground & Nico
(Verve, 1967)

By David Sprague

You can't spell party without "arty." Andy Warhol may have never spoken that exact phrase, but the philosophy permeated virtually every aspect of his public life, and nowhere more vividly than in the days of the Exploding Plastic Inevitable, the prehistoric rave that launched the Velvet Underground into the consciousness of socialites and tastemakers across . . . well, across a select swath of New York City.

For all their dark and stormy accoutrements, the embryonic Velvets were primarily a dance band—heck, Lou Reed was just a few years removed from a career crafting not-quite-nation-sweeping dance crazes like "The Ostrich" (which he recorded in 1965 as part of the studio aggregation, the Primitives). That visceral attitude is evident in virtually every groove of their debut album *The Velvet Underground & Nico*.

Sure, the disc is packed with songs about sadomasochism, opiates, and dissipated poets, and it's peppered with appearances by a German ice queen, but at its core, it's as much a testament to the fine art of booty-moving as anything by George Clinton—although Reed and his cohorts were admittedly more interested in twisting rather than freeing the minds attached to the asses that would eventually follow.

That has a bit to do with Reed's thrumming, hypnotic guitar wash—legend has it that he specially customized his guitar, sanding off a passel of frets in order to achieve the dislocating, vaguely Eastern effect that swirls through tunes such as "Venus In Furs" and "The Black Angel's Death Song"—as well as Sterling Morrison's churning, R&B-rooted rhythm-guitar playing (poured into a suit, the Long Islander could've passed muster in Muscle Shoals). The most effective tool in the band's kit, however, was the upturned bass drum placed before drummer Moe Tucker, whose unblinking adherence to minimalist form—and refusal to work gizmos as superfluous as cymbals or standard drum sticks—confounded the technique-obsessed while cementing her rep as the Mondrian of the mallets.

The Velvets didn't, of course, live by primitivism alone. If they had, they'd have been little more than a higher-brow answer to garage-dwelling peers like, say, the Sonics. Warhol's endorsement—and the vaguely sitophiliac, banana-emblazoned sleeve he designed for *The Velvet Underground & Nico*—was only the first indication that opposable thumbs were fully operational here. The more

The Velvet Underground & Nico, North American mono issue cover.

The Velvet Underground & Nico, North American mono issue cover with the contested photograph of Eric Emerson. The band photograph was taken by Factory photographer Nat Finkelstein, who explained that the Emerson image was laid over his photo by Paul Morrissey to make a collage.

significant steps up the evolutionary ladder were charted by John Cale, who picked up an affinity for drones from experimental icon La Monte Young and a fondness for button-pushing from generations of acerbic Welsh ancestors.

Cale's expressionist slashing didn't exactly send droves of kids running for viola lessons with visions of rock stardom dancing in their heads, but the keening tenor of pieces such as "The Black Angel's Death Song" and "European Son" (which interpolated found-sound violence more effectively than any tune since "The Leader of the Pack") did permanently broaden rock's sonic palette, for better and worse. His fire—the kind one might find in a coal furnace glowing in the bowels of a dusky factory—contrasts starkly with the ice that follows in the wake of Nico's troika of appearances.

The pros and cons of Nico's presence on the album have long been debated. Ultimately her deadpan delivery and dead-eyed demeanor made for a breathtakingly blank canvas, a notion driven home most effectively in "I'll Be Your Mirror," an unblinking sublimation of self that stands as a sort of bookend to the more blatant Domina/submissive dynamic conveyed in "Venus In Furs." There's considerably less meat—and just as little motion—to her best-known turn in the spotlight: "Femme Fatale" could just as easily have trickled out a decade earlier as a Julie London album track, but for the two minutes and fourteen seconds it occupies on this album, the Warholian aesthetic flawlessly adopts a sonic form.

Reed didn't entirely share that aesthetic, but he did seem to find a similar solace in detachment—though he wrote of arriving at the void by a different route than Warhol, who emptied himself into the gaping maw of what would later be codified as trash culture (and, as an equal and opposite reaction, absorbed the trashiest stuff he could find into his own marrow). Neither Marilyn Monroe nor the Campbell's Soup Kids quite did the trick for Reed, however. His quest for nothingness took a more direct route—one that stopped at the pre-gentrified East Harlem corner of Lexington and 125th.

While the Beats had explored junkie life pretty extensively in the previous decade—Jack Gelber's 1959 play *The Connection*, which a *New York Times* reviewer dubbed "a farrago of dirt," was a clear precursor to "I'm Waiting For The Man"—there was something undeniably unsettling about the ambivalence with which Reed delivered his opiated odes. The Velvets stopped short of "Drinkin' Wine Spo-Dee-O-Dee"-style celebrations of sticking a spike into one's vein, but the evenness in Reed's voice when he ponders self-nullification defies the listener to find a whit of regret about the descent into the maelstrom.

Oddly, remorse—not to mention a healthy dose of paranoia—only takes center-stage on the album's most seemingly bucolic offering, "Sunday Morning," a song that, dislocatingly enough, opens the proceedings with what could well be a look back on all the synapse-buffeting experiences that follow. Its gauziness, punctuated by Cale's chiming celeste playing, conveys the act of walking on egg shells ("Watch out," Reed intones, "the world's behind you") inherent in trying to piece together the forgotten debris of a Saturday night like the one abstracted in "Run Run Run."

Forgotten pieces and empty spaces weren't the primary building blocks of rock 'n' roll at the time the Velvet Underground and Nico recorded these eleven songs, but more than four decades on, they've proven to be more impervious to the ravages of time than the era's more concrete artifacts. And no matter how many times one takes the "peel slowly and see" challenge posed on the original album sleeve, there's always something new to discover.

> "It's an extremely pretty sexy banana, and the album cover peels, which is nice, to reveal the inside of a very sexy, groovy banana."
>
> —Lou Reed, quoted in Steven Watson's *Factory Made: Warhol and the Sixties*, 2003

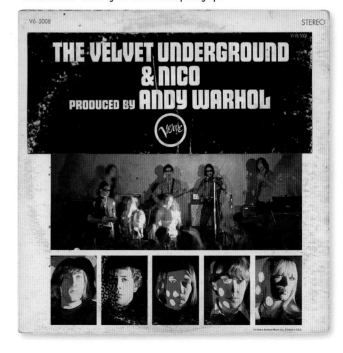

The Velvet Underground & Nico, North American stereo issue cover with the "lawsuit sticker" covering the Eric Emerson photograph.

"Andy Warhol was familiar with the strategies for creating homoerotic images that remained within the law. Physique magazines and movies used images that were homoerotically doubled entendres. Most of them were not hard to understand; a classic featured a man eating a banana."

Steven Watson, *Factory Made: Warhol and the Sixties*, 2003

At a 2006 Chelsea Street yard sale in New York City passerby Warren Hill stumbled upon this Velvet Underground acetate. He bought the record for 75 cents and took it home. The acetate turned out to be original tracks of what would become *The Velvet Underground & Nico* straight from the band's first sessions at Scepter Studios under the supervision of producer Norman Dolph. Four tracks were alternate takes, including "Heroin," "European Son," "Venus In Furs," and "I'm Waiting For The Man." The remaining five tracks were in alternate mixes: "Femme Fatale," "The Black Angel's Death Song," "All Tomorrow's Parties," "I'll Be Your Mirror," and "Run Run Run." Hill later sold the acetate on eBay for $25,000.

LIVE PERFORMANCES AND REHEARSALS 1965–1967 BY OLIVIER LANDEMAINE

Spring 1965: "The Launching of the Dream Weapon," Film-Makers' Cinemathèque, New York City. Mixed-media stage presentation organized by Piero Heliczer with Reed, Cale, MacLise, and Morrison playing music behind the screen. Other similar performances took place during summer 1965. Heliczer taped music played during some of those performances.

November 1965: *The Making of an Underground Film*, New York City. Making of Piero Heliczer's *Venus In Furs* movie for CBS News' Walter Cronkite show, broadcast late December 1965, and featuring Cale, Morrison, and Reed playing "Heroin," with Heliczer joining in on saxophone.

December 4–5, 1965: "The Rites of the Dream Weapon," Film-Makers' Cinemathèque, New York City. Mixed-media stage presentation.

December 11, 1965: Summit High School Auditorium, Summit, NJ. First show with the name "the Velvet Underground" and with Maureen Tucker. Triple bill with the Myddle Class as headliners and the Forty Fingers as cosupport. This opening was offered by the legendary journalist Al Aronowitz, who was also the Myddle Class' manager.

Mid-December 1965: Café Bizarre, Greenwich Village, New York City

January 3, 1966: Rehearsals at the Factory, New York City

January 13, 1966: Annual Dinner of the New York Society for Clinical Psychiatry at Delmonico's Hotel, New York City. First public appearance with Nico.

February 7, 1966: *USA Artists* TV show, on WNET, New York City. Featuring Andy Warhol, who introduces the Velvet Underground.

February 8–13, 1966: Andy Warhol, Up-Tight at Film-Makers' Cinemathèque, New York City

March 7, 1966: Rehearsal before Exploding Plastic Inevitable, the Factory, New York City

March 9, 1966: Rutgers Up-Tight, Rutgers University, NJ

March 12, 1966: Up-Tight with Andy Warhol, University of Michigan Film Festival, Ann Arbor, MI

March 1966: Paraphernalia Store, New York City

March 31, 1966: "April Fool Dance & Models Ball," Village Gate, New York City

April 1966: 20th anniversary party for the *Paris Review*, Village Gate, New York City

April 1–30, 1966: Exploding Plastic Inevitable, the Dom, East Village, New York City

April 26, 1966: NOW Festival, National Roller Skating Arena, Washington, D.C.

April 27, 1966: Film-Makers' Cinemathèque, New York City

May 3–5, 1966: Exploding Plastic Inevitable, the Trip, West Hollywood, CA. The engagement was May 3–18, but the club was closed after the third night.

May 27–29, 1966: Exploding Plastic Inevitable, Fillmore Auditorium, San Francisco, CA

June 21–July 3, 1966: Exploding Plastic Inevitable, Poor Richard's, Chicago, IL. These shows were without Reed, who was at New York's Beth Israel Hospital for hepatitis, and without Nico, who took off for Ibiza at the beginning of June. Angus MacLise was on drums, Maureen on bass, Sterling and John on vocals. The engagement—originally June 21–26—was held over to July 3.

Summer/Fall 1966: *The Velvet Underground And Nico: A Symphony Of Sound*, the Factory, New York City. Filmed by Warhol.

August 31–September 4, 1966: Exploding Plastic Inevitable, Chrysler Art Museum, Provincetown, MA

October 1966: Exploding Plastic Inevitable, Balloon Farm (formerly the Dom), New York City. The engagement may have begun in late September.

October 29, 1966: Exploding Plastic Inevitable, Institute of Contemporary Arts, Boston, MA

October 30, 1966: "Halloween Mod Happening," Exploding Plastic Inevitable, Leicester Airport, Leicester, MA

November 3, 1966: Exploding Plastic Inevitable, Topper Club, Cincinnati, OH

November 3, 1966: Exploding Plastic Inevitable, Music Hall's Ballroom, Cincinnati, OH

November 4, 1966: Exploding Plastic Inevitable, Valleydale Ballroom, Columbus, OH

November 5, 1966: Exploding Plastic Inevitable, University of West Virginia, Wheeling, WV

November 6, 1966: Exploding Plastic Inevitable, Masonic Auditorium, Cleveland, OH

November 12, 1966: Exploding Plastic Inevitable, McMaster University, Hamilton, Ontario, Canada

November 17–20, 1966: Dick Clark's "Caravan of Stars Tour," Exploding Plastic Inevitable, Michigan State Fair Coliseum, Highland Park, MI

November 20, 1966: "World's First Mod Wedding Happening," Carnaby Street Fun Festival, Michigan State Fairgrounds, Highland Park, MI

December 4, 1966: *Night Beat* magazine presents Freak Out '66, Action House, Island Park, NY

December 10–11, 1966: Philadelphia Art Festival, YMHA Auditorium, Philadelphia, PA

January 2–14, 1967: "The Steve Paul & Andy Warhol Underground Amateur Hour," Steve Paul's Scene, New York City

January 16–23, 1967: Montréal Worlds Fair, Montréal, Quebec, Canada

February 18, 1967: "NY Relief Fun Glitter Acidheadspeed Ball & Parade," Film-Makers' Cinemathèque, New York City

March 15–22, 1967: The Balloon Farm, New York City

March 31–April 1, 1967: Exploding Plastic Inevitable, Rhode Island School of Design, Providence, RI

April 7–8, 1967: The Gymnasium, New York City

April 9, 1967: "A Night Of Andy Warhol," Hill Auditorium, Ann Arbor, MI

April 11, 1967: Cheetah, New York City

April 14–16, 21–23 & 28–30, 1967: Exploding Plastic Inevitable, the Gymnasium, New York City

April 1967: Marwick Theater, Ann Arbor, MI

May 1967: Exploding Plastic Inevitable, Steve Paul's Scene, New York City. This was the final Exploding Plastic Inevitable show.

May 26–27, 1967: The Boston Tea Party, Boston, MA

June 9–10, 1967: The Boston Tea Party, Boston, MA

July 3–6, 1967: The A-Go-Go, West Yarmouth, Cape Cod, MA

July 19–22 & 26–29, 1967: The Trauma, Philadelphia, PA

July 1967: Benefit for Merce Cunningham at Philip Johnson Glass House, New Canaan, CT

August 11–12, 1967: The Boston Tea Party, Boston, MA

September 22–24, 1967: Savoy Theatre, Boston, MA

December 20, 1967: The Cinematheque Coffeehouse Palace of Pleasure, San Francisco, CA

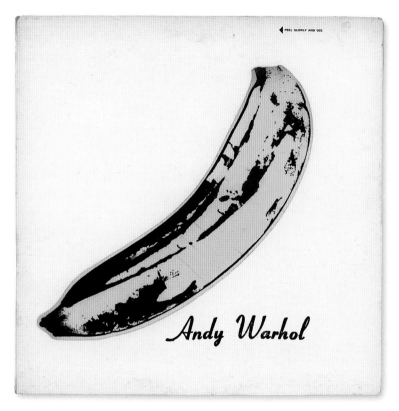

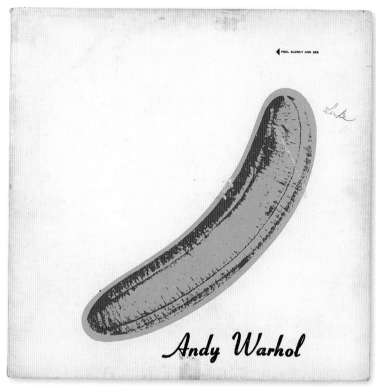

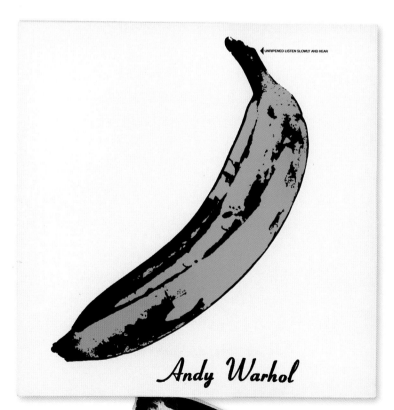

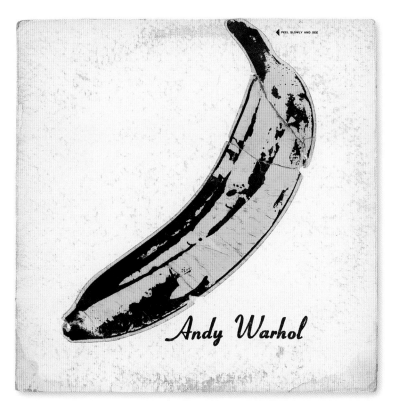

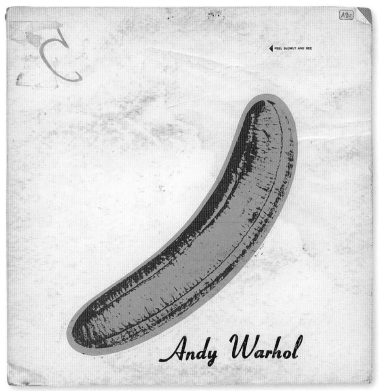

WHIP IT ON ME, JIM: FROM "SISTER RAY" TO "JESUS"

"How do you define a group who moved from 'Heroin' to 'Jesus' in two short years? It is not enough to say that they have one of the broadest ranges of any group extant; this should be apparent to anyone who has listened closely to their three albums. The real question is what this music is about—smack, meth, deviate sex, and drugdreams, or something deeper?"

—Lester Bangs on the Velvet Underground in *Rolling Stone*, May 17, 1969

John Cale contends that Lou Reed had been shopping around for a new manager for a year before the Velvets formally broke from Andy Warhol and signed with Boston-based hustler Steve Sesnick, none too fondly recalled by the Welshman as "a real snake" and "a miserable piece of trash." The group toured through much of the second half of 1967, pausing in September to enter New York's Mayfair Sound Studios with producer Tom Wilson and engineer Gary Kellgren to lay down a new set of material, some of which had been coming together since the summer a year earlier. This time the musicians were determined to record as quickly as possible with a minimum of studio polish, the better to capture the power of their live performances.

"There's a lot of improvisation on *White Light/White Heat*," Cale writes in *What's Welsh for Zen.* "Most of the

"Roughly speaking, every creep, every degenerate, every hustler, booster, and rip-off artist, every wasted weirdo packed up his or her clap, crabs, and cons and headed off to the Promised Land. This sleazy legion . . . then descended upon the hapless hippies (and their dupes) in San Francisco. But behind them in Manhattan, all was suddenly quiet, clean, and beautiful—like the world of Noah after the Flood. And so at the height of the 'Summer of Love' we stayed in NYC and recorded *White Light/White Heat*, an orgasm of our own."

—Sterling Morrison, quoted in Steven Watson's *Factory Made: Warhol and the Sixties*, 2003

The Velvet Underground plays Vancouver's Retinal Circus on July 30, 1968, and again from October 31 through November 3, 1968. From left: Lou Reed, Maureen Tucker, Sterling Morrison, and John Cale. *Rick McGrath*

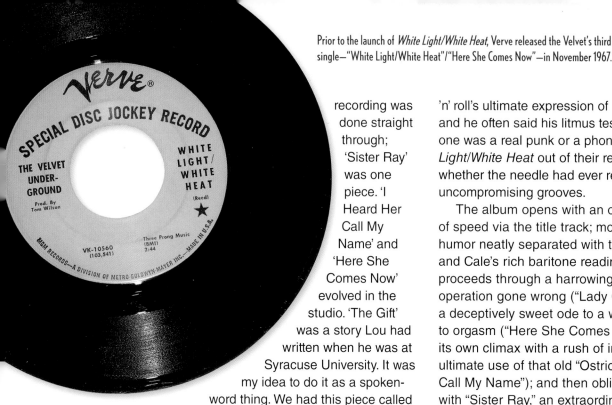

Prior to the launch of *White Light/White Heat*, Verve released the Velvet's third single—"White Light/White Heat"/"Here She Comes Now"—in November 1967.

recording was done straight through; 'Sister Ray' was one piece. 'I Heard Her Call My Name' and 'Here She Comes Now' evolved in the studio. 'The Gift' was a story Lou had written when he was at Syracuse University. It was my idea to do it as a spoken-word thing. We had this piece called

> "We wanted to go as high and as hard as we could."
>
> —Lou Reed, quoted in Steven Watson's *Factory Made: Warhol and the Sixties*, 2003

'Booker T' that was an instrumental, so instead of wasting it we decided to combine them. . . . We were intent on recording this album live in the studio because we were so good live at this point. We played and played and played, and to keep that animalism there, we insisted on playing at the volume that we played onstage."

Released on January 30, 1968, *White Light/White Heat* is in many ways Cale's album—or at least the ultimate realization, recording flaws aside, of his ideas from the classical avant-garde colliding with Reed's extraordinary abilities for lyrical improvisation. Lester Bangs called it "rock 'n' roll's ultimate expression of nihilism and destruction," and he often said his litmus test for whether or not someone was a real punk or a phony was that he'd pull *White Light/White Heat* out of their record collection and see whether the needle had ever really spent much time in its uncompromising grooves.

The album opens with an ode to the chemical rush of speed via the title track; moves into a bit of twisted humor neatly separated with the music in one channel and Cale's rich baritone reading in the other ("The Gift"); proceeds through a harrowing tale of a transsexual operation gone wrong ("Lady Godiva's Operation") and a deceptively sweet ode to a woman who seems unable to orgasm ("Here She Comes Now"); begins to build to its own climax with a rush of insanity and the band's ultimate use of that old "Ostrich guitar" ("I Heard Her Call My Name"); and then obliterates everything else with "Sister Ray," an extraordinary seventeen-minute, twenty-seven-second sonic assault coupled with a Reed lyric telling a story that could have come from *Last Exit to Brooklyn*.

"It has eight characters in it and this guy gets killed and nobody does anything," Reed said of the lyrics to "Sister Ray" in a 2002 interview with *The Stranger*. "The situation is a bunch of drag queens taking some sailors home with them, shooting up on smack, and having this orgy when the police appear." Years earlier he described the music to Bangs as a "jam [that] came about right there in the studio—we didn't use any splices or anything. I had been listening to a lot of Cecil Taylor and Ornette Coleman and wanted to get something like that with a rock 'n' roll feeling. And I think we were successful, but I also think that we carried that about as far as we could for our abilities as a band that was basically rock 'n' roll. Later, we continued to play that kind of music and I was really experimenting a lot with guitar, but most of the audiences in the clubs just weren't receptive to it at all."

Indeed, the commercial reception for the band's second album was even bleaker than it had been for its predecessor: *White Light/White Heat* spent exactly two weeks on the Billboard chart at 199, and then it vanished for good.

[continued on 114]

> "It was a very rabid record. The first one had some gentility, some beauty. The second one was consciously anti-beauty."
>
> —John Cale, quoted in Steven Watson's *Factory Made: Warhol and the Sixties*, 2003

> "What we were trying to do was to really fry the tracks."
>
> —Sterling Morrison

THE ABOVE-GROUND SOUND OF THE VELVET UNDERGROUND

The Velvet Underground's velvet, leather, satin, and brass stuff was designed by Betsey Johnson of Paraphernalia.

We always get a thrill when a great underground rock group finally breaks through the surface to full-fledged popularity. And we get an even bigger thrill when the group in question happens to be the Velvet Underground.

Spurred to semi-fame, underground style, by Andy Warhol in his Dom days, the Velvet Underground have been laboring in the murky depths for far too long. Now, with the advent of their sensational new album, "White Light/White Heat" (Verve), that problem has been solved, once and for all.

Welcome to the hot glare of fame, fortune, and publicity, group! HULLABALOO gives its first happening party in honor of the four valiant Velvets: Lou Reed (vocals, lead guitar, piano), John Cale (vocals, electric viola, bass guitar), Sterling Morrison (vocals, guitar, bass guitar), and Maureen Tucker (drums).

Happy sunshine!

Photos by Ralph Garcia

56 HULLABALOO

Advertisement, *White Light/White Heat.*

> "There was fantastic leakage because everyone was playing so loud and we had so much electronic junk with us in the studio—all these fuzzers and compressors. Gary Kellgren, the engineer, who is ultra-competent, told us repeatedly, 'You can't do it—all the needles are on red.' And we reacted as we always reacted: 'Look, we don't know what goes on in there and we don't want to hear about it. Just do the best you can.' And so the album is all fuzzy, there's all that white noise. . . . We wanted to do something electronic and energetic. We had the energy and the electronics, but we didn't know that it couldn't be recorded."
>
> —Sterling Morrison, quoted in Clinton Heylin's *From the Velvets to the Voidoids,* 1993

MGM/Polydor European compilation two-LP album set, combining *The Velvet Underground & Nico* and *White Light/White Heat.*

Andy Warhol's *Velvet Underground* featuring *Nico*

MGM
2683 006 SELECT

YOU'VE NEVER SEEN A CONTEST LIKE THIS! THE VELVET UNDERGROUND-VERVE RECORDS DESIGN YOUR OWN PSYCHEDELIC SUBWAY TOKEN CONTEST!

1st Prize: 5 MGM Play Tape Machines
2nd Prize: Next 200 Winners Get Velvet Underground LPs
3rd Prize: Next 300 Winners Get Velvet Underground 45s

What you see above is a blank subway token—a free trip on the Velvet Underground! All you have to do to win this contest is to fill in the token—with crayons, oils, watercolors—in the psychedelic way! Most-colorful, best-designed tokens win the prizes. Start now. Enter as many times as you like. All entries MUST be on official entry blanks. Contest closes midnight May 25, 1968.

OFFICIAL ENTRY BLANK

Mail to: Velvet Underground
HULLABALOO
201 E. 42nd Street
New York, N.Y. 10017

Name _____

Address _____ Age _____

City _____ State _____ Zip _____

Contest advertisement from *Hullabaloo* magazine promoting *White Light/White Heat.*

109

A Joyful Noise?

The Termite Art Appeal of
White Light/White Heat (Verve, 1968)

By Glenn Kenny

Forbidding—that's a reasonably apt word to describe how the Velvet Underground's second LP, *White Light/ White Heat*, must have come off to rock record buyers upon its not-too-terribly heralded release in the early days of 1968. First off, there was the front cover: the album's title, the record company (Verve's) logo, and the band name in one line of white type (a compressed variant of the very modern Helvetica Neue, it looks like) across the top of a field of black. Or so it seemed: The earliest versions of the cover were printed with a black-on-black rendering of a skull tattoo that you had to tilt the album to a certain angle to discern. Cheerier and cheerier. The back cover was a solarized black-and-white portrait of the band, half its four members—drummer Maureen Tucker and violist/keyboardist/bassist John Cale—hiding behind sunglasses. A third member, guitarist and bassist Sterling Morrison, has got his bangs in his eyes, and the fourth, lead singer and guitarist Lou Reed—well, his orbs are sunk so deep, he resembles a hipster version of the undead Imhotep played by Boris Karloff in 1932's *The Mummy*. So, not the friendliest-looking bunch.

Things did not get less intimidating once you put the needle on the record: Buzzing guitar, roiling bass, a primitive pounding cymbal beat . . . and anachronistic harmony vocals and boogie-woogie piano. All of which seemed submerged beneath an icy sheet of noise. This music wasn't just hard to listen to—it was hard to actually *hear*. And it only got more extreme from there, with about two minutes of lyrical—but sinister—respite at the end of side one. Side two yields an explosion of tension-wire electric guitar, followed by the most committed noise jam ever perpetrated by a rock and roll group, almost twenty minutes' worth of it.

Then there was the subject matter of the songs. In order: "White Light/White Heat," a snarky paean to amphetamine abuse, containing the promise that such practice could lead to oedipal murder; "The Gift," a short story (literally) about a collegiate "schmuck"—his putative girlfriend's term—who attempts to mail himself to said girlfriend, with bloody disastrous results; "Lady Godiva's Operation," in which the imperious, debauched lady of the title is subjected to surgical butchery; "Here She Comes Now," the above-cited spot of respite, about a girl who's "made out of wood"; "I Heard Her Call My Name," in which

White Light/White Heat, North American issue cover, designed by Andy Warhol from a photo by Billy Name.

White Light/White Heat, Great Britain and European issue cover, here signed by John Cale.

the singer swears his dead lover spoke to him, and then suffers a breakdown; and "Sister Ray," the noise jam, a rambling, nodded-out account of sex and murder among junkies and transvestites.

It's hardly any wonder that the word "nihilist" is thrown around so often when the Velvet Underground comes up: There's a very real sense in which *White Light/White Heat* tells the listener that it doesn't need him or her. But that lack of need doesn't have to be interpreted negatively. That is to say, not needing you is not the same as rejecting you. And the fact is, *White Light/White Heat* is best approached, to paraphrase Albert Camus, by imagining the Velvet Underground happy.

Because, in fact, when they were making the album, the musicians *were* happy. Honed into a finely tuned noise-and-drone-groove machine by months of touring, beginning to establish an identity apart from that of a hip accoutrement to Andy Warhol's Pop-Art caravan, the Velvet Underground went into the studio in the fall of 1967 as a band eager to strut its stuff. "We were intent on recording this album live in the studio because we were so good live at this point. We played and played and played, and to keep that animalism there, we insisted on playing at the volume that we played on stage," John Cale recalls in his autobiography, *What's Welsh for Zen*. Unfortunately, the band's putative support system couldn't keep up with it. Producer Tom Wilson, who also oversaw the band's debut, could be either a hands-on or hands-off producer, depending on the circumstances—he conceived the electric backing track that made Simon and Garfunkel's "The Sound of Silence" a radio hit, but let Frank Zappa keep his head for the Mothers of Invention's opening salvo *Freak Out!*—and he was perhaps a bit too laissez-faire in this case, letting the band blast away with no regard for the limitations of the recording equipment taking it all down. "We were working in a very small studio with no isolation so it was all this noise just smashing into more noise, but we felt that if we caught the excitement of a live performance on tape we'd have achieved our aim," Cale recalls. "We never quite realized that there were technical problems in turning everything past nine." The late Sterling Morrison, interviewed for Clinton Heylin's book *From the Velvets to the Voidoids*, said, "We wanted to do something electronic and energetic. We had the energy and the electronics, but we didn't know that it couldn't be recorded. . . . What we were trying to do was to really fry the tracks."

And fry they did, to the extent that even all the sophisticated digital technology that went into remastering the Velvets' oeuvre for the CD box set *Peel Slowly and See*

cannot quite pull the record from the sonic murk wherein some details are aggressively foregrounded—Reed's third-rail guitar on "I Heard Her Call My Name," which surely warrants its spotlight—and others are all but buried; witness Cale's delicate viola arpeggios on "Here She Comes Now." But what comes through at all times is the band's dedication to making what the film critic Manny Farber called "termite art." Termite art, Farber said, "feels its way through walls of particularization, with no sign that the artist has any object in mind other than eating away the immediate boundaries of his art." It "leaves nothing in its path other than the signs of its eager, industrious, unkempt activity."

Ignoring the feel-good sentimentality of the summer of 1967 and purveying a radicalism that would have nothing to do with the feel-bad extremes of the months and years to come, these termites would prove themselves among the most industrious artists of their time. 🕶

Advertisement, *White Light/White Heat.*

Advertisement, the Boston Tea Party,
Boston, Massachusetts, August 11–12, 1967.

Advertisement, the Boston Tea Party,
Boston, Massachusetts, May 16–18, 1968.

The Velvet Underground performs on its own, without Andy Warhol's entourage, during spring 1967
at the Boston Tea Party. *Billy Name/Ovoworks/Time Life Pictures/Getty Images*

[continued from 108]

Undaunted, the band forged ahead, performing on the road whenever it could through 1968; the group had decided to boycott New York because of the lack of radio support, and because it had lost its ideal venue when Bob Dylan's manager Albert Grossman swooped in, stole the Dom, and rechristened it the Balloon Farm while the Exploding Plastic Inevitable made its first trip to California. Reed, Cale, and Morrison had stopped living together in their communal band crash pad in late 1967, and now, the more time they spent touring, the more their personalities clashed. Cale hated Sesnick, and in their version of the classic Paul McCartney/John Lennon/Yoko Ono band melodrama, Reed resented

Cale's girlfriend, designer Betsey Johnson, whom he married in April 1968.

Reed, Cale, Morrison, and Tucker entered the studio twice in 1968 in an attempt to cut a single, but the results illustrated the growing chasm in the band between the direction Reed wanted to take and the one that Cale wished to pursue. In February, at A&R Studios in New York, the group recorded Reed's lighthearted and upbeat rocker "Temptation Inside Your Heart" and the lovely "Stephanie Says," while in May, at T.T.G. Studios in Los Angeles, it laid down the droning "Hey Mr. Rain." The latter, officially unreleased until decades later, would be Cale's last studio contribution.

[continued on 120]

Shrine Exposition Hall, 32nd & Figueroa - Visuals by: Single wing turquoise bird.   Time: 8:30 p.m. to 2:00 a.m.
Tickets available at: Wallichs Music City Stores , Mutual Ticket Agencies, Free Press Bookstores,
Potpourri, Either or Bookstores, Sound Spectrun in LAGUNA Beach. Price: $3.00 in advance -- $3.50 at the door

Time: 8:30 p.m. to 2:00 a.m.
Visuals by: Single wing turquoise bird.

Poster, Avalon Ballroom, San Francisco, California, June 7-9, 1968. Artist: Bob Schnepf/Family Dog Productions

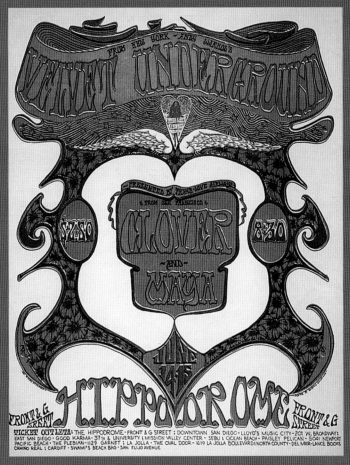

Poster, Hippodrome, San Diego, California, June 14–15, 1968.
Artist: Rebecca Galdeano

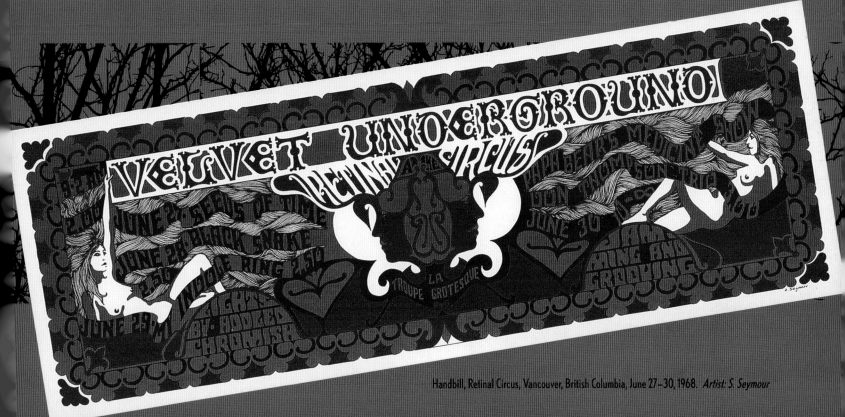

Handbill, Retinal Circus, Vancouver, British Columbia, June 27–30, 1968. *Artist: S. Seymour*

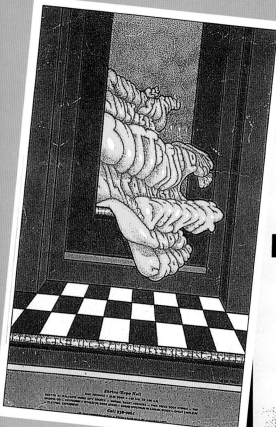

PINNACLE DANCE

BUTTERFIELD BLUES BAND
VELVET UNDERGROUND
SLY & FAMILY STONE
ROCKETS • 8 P.M. - 2 A.M.
JULY 12-13

THIS FRI. & SAT. - SHRINE HALL
32ND & FIGUEROA OFF HARBOR FWY. AT EXPOSITION

TICKETS: ALL MUSIC CITY STORES, MUTUAL AGENCIES, FREE PRESS BOOK-STORES, GROOVE COMPANY, PHINIUS, POTPOURRI, MAGIC THEATRE, EITHER/-OR BOOKSTORE, SOUND SPECTRUM, AND AT THE DOOR. PINNACLE INFORMA-TION CALL 938-0061.

LIGHTS BY SINGLE WING TURQUOISE BIRD

Poster and handbill, Avalon Ballroom, San Francisco, California, July 19–21, 1968. *Artist: Family Dog Productions*

[continued from 114]

In September, on the eve of a trip to Cleveland, Reed met with Tucker and Morrison to tell them that Cale was out. The onerous task of informing Cale fell to Morrison. "Lou always got other people to do his dirty work for him," Cale said. In the many years since their split, neither man has earned a reputation for playing nicely with others—quite the opposite—and in retrospect their break perhaps was inevitable, though it cannot be denied that each brought something uniquely powerful out of the other, and neither has quite matched it since. "It was never the same for me after John left," Morrison said. "He was not easy to replace. . . . We moved more towards unanimity of opinion [and] I don't think that's a good thing. I always thought that what made us good were the tensions and oppositions. Bands that fight together make better music."

To replace Cale, Reed turned to another Long Island native five years his junior, Doug Yule, who'd migrated to Boston to play in a band called the Grass Menagerie; that group's managers were friendly with Sesnick, who made the connection to the Velvets. Though he lacked Cale's vision, Yule was a natural musician: "My reason for being in music was a hunger—I couldn't have *not* been in music," he said. Of equal importance to Reed, Yule wouldn't compete in an attempt to try to lead the band: He simply was a useful tool, the first of many that Reed would utilize in the years to come.

"We would spend time together, where he would take out these songs that he was fooling around with and ask for help: 'I'm thinking about this melody, what's a chord that goes with that?'" Yule told Pat Thomas in a 1995 interview for *Perfect Sound Forever*. "He'd ask for help

In September 1968, Lou Reed informed Sterling Morrison and Moe Tucker that John Cale was out of the band. In Cale's place arrived Doug Yule, a young guitarist-bassist-vocalist who would follow Reed's dictates. From left: Morrison, Reed, Tucker, and Yule. *Polygram Records Archives*

building things, then he would return six months later with the song put together and announce it: 'Here's my new tune.'"

With Yule on bass and organ, the band moved from the chaos and noise of the Cale years to an emphasis on relentless rhythm in Reed's more driving songs ("What Goes On," "Beginning To See The Light") and a quiet, beautiful fragility in his slower ballads ("Candy Says," inspired by Factory Superstar and pre-op transsexual Candy Darling, and "Pale Blue Eyes," written in the midst of a rekindled romance with a Syracuse-era girlfriend). The only evidence of the wild experimentation of the first two albums would come in "The Murder Mystery," a stream-of-consciousness assault of words and music that featured all four band members on vocals. It was only partly successful: "Good try, but it didn't work," Reed concluded.

The band recorded its self-titled third album at T.T.G. in November and December 1968. By all accounts these sessions were much easier and more pleasant, though Morrison and Tucker were angry when Reed remixed some of the songs shortly before the final release in March 1969; they contended that the original mixes were better, and Morrison called Reed's claustrophobic version "the closet mix."

The group also seemed concerned if not apologetic to be releasing a relatively mellow album that stood in such stark contrast to its predecessor, and Reed and Morrison invented the tale that its quiet sound was the result of their effects pedals having been stolen at the airport. "I don't know where [that story] came from, unless it was started to make the group more interesting somehow," Yule told *Perfect Sound Forever*. "That's just what we were playing then—we were playing much more melodic stuff."

Slowly but surely the nascent rock press was growing more enthusiastic about the band—in addition to Bangs and Goldstein, its core of champions now included Ellen Willis, Richard Meltzer, Richard Cromelin, and *Crawdaddy* founder Paul Williams—and the band was starting to move in a direction more in step with the times. Even critics who didn't completely get it were beginning to appreciate what the band was doing; in

Poster, the Boston Tea Party, Boston, Massachusetts, December 12–14, 1968. *Artist: Steve Nelson*

his list of the best albums of 1969 for the *Chicago Tribune*, Robb Baker gave *The Velvet Underground* an honorable mention, placing it behind a number of admittedly worthy contenders (*Let It Bleed* by the Rolling Stones, *Tommy* by the Who, *Abbey Road* by the Beatles, and *River Deep, Mountain High* by Ike and Tina Turner) as well as some that were not nearly so deserving (*Hand Sown, Home Grown* by Linda Ronstadt, *Stay with Me* by Lorraine Ellison, and *Illuminations* by Buffy Sainte-Marie).

The album was greeted nonetheless with the usual commercial hostility, and, more troubling, the band was starting to endure an increasing indifference bordering on animosity from its own record company, now led by Mike Curb, a conservative Republican businessman and ally of President Richard M. Nixon in his war on drugs. As he began to remake the label in his own square image, Curb issued a corporate manifesto: "Groups that are associated with hard drugs . . . are very undependable. They're difficult to work with, and they're hard on your sales and marketing people." The Velvets' days as an MGM act clearly were numbered.

[*continued on 132*]

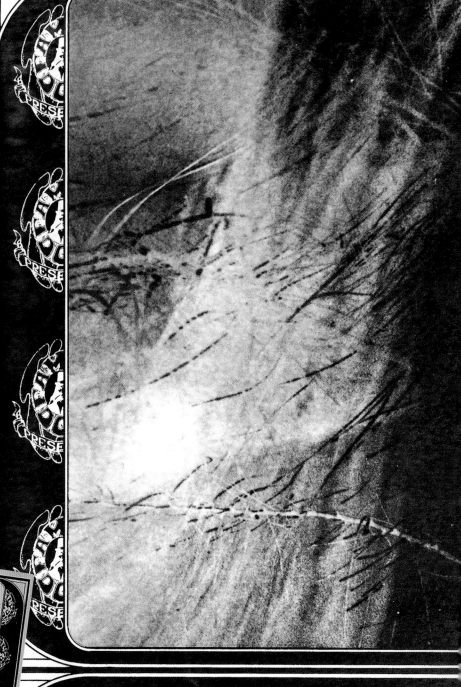

Poster and handbill, Avalon Ballroom, San Francisco, California, October 18–20, 1968. *Artist: San Francisco Poster Co.*

JEFFERSON AIRPLANE · CAPT· BEEFHEART

SUTTER AT VAN NESS

iN SAN FRANCiSCO

AVALON BALLROOM

N FRANCISCO: TOWER RECORDS (COLUMBUS & BAY), GRAMOPHONE STORES (ALL), CITY
BEACH), THE TOWN SQUIRE (1318 POLK), MNASIDIKA (HAIGHT ASHBURY), XANADU (HAIGHT
ISCOUNT RECORDS SAUSALITO: TIDES BOOKSTORE SAN RAFAEL: RECORD KING SAN MATEO:
EL CAMINO), TOWN & COUNTRY MUSIC (4TH & EL CAMINO) REDWOOD CITY: REDWOOD
WINSLOW) MENLO PARK: KEPLER'S BOOKS (825 EL CAMINO) PALO ALTO: EAST FARTHING
PER) SAN JOSE: DISCORAMA (237 S. FIRST ST.), DISCOUNT RECORDS (VALLEY FAIR).

ILL · SUN · GRAFFIX · Box 236 · Lagunitas · California   *Photo: Bellmer Wright*   SAN FRANCISCO POSTER CO.

"The Pretty Stuff"
The Calmative Side of *The Velvet Underground* (MGM, 1969)

By Rob O'Connor

It's said that in order to know if you really love someone—really *love* them—you must see them at their worst and decide if you can love them at that moment. If their weaknesses can be seen as strengths, together you become something greater than the sum of your parts. No band understood this better than the Velvet Underground, which was both bound and set free by its limitations. The band members routinely turned minuses into plusses: Lou Reed's paltry vocal range; Maureen Tucker's primal rhythmic skills; Sterling Morrison's modest, almost reluctant, anti-guitar solos; and their inevitable out-of-stepness. It's no surprise that with the departure of John Cale, the band's most accomplished musician and the one who defined much of its avant-garde reputation, the group went in a new direction as if it had always been part of the plan. In retrospect, the soft purring of its self-titled third album *is* the logical counterweight to the feedback-overload of their second. Had Cale stuck around, he wouldn't have had much to do.

"We did the third album deliberately as anti-production," Morrison said. "It sounds like it was done in a closet—it's flat, and that's the way we wanted it. The songs are very quiet and it's kind of insane."

Like each of its studio albums, *The Velvet Underground* became an influential touchstone. From the nightmarish self-loathings of Alex Chilton with Big Star's *Third* (which included a collapsing version of "Femme Fatale") to the smooth sadcore of Dean Wareham's career with Galaxie 500 and Luna, the contemplative ponderings of Mark Kozelek with Red House Painters and Sun Kil Moon, and even the "emo" strains of Death Cab for Cutie, the Velvets' third album provided a blueprint for bands that had the blues but didn't necessarily want to play them.

Cale's replacement, Doug Yule, slotted right in, the right man at the right time, singing the album's opening number "Candy Says" and falling behind Reed for harmonies and bass lines that never challenge the status quo. With his archnemesis, or at least his most vocal dissident, removed from the picture, Reed co-opted the band as his backing group. "Cale's departure allowed Lou Reed's sensitive, meaningful side to hold sway," Morrison said. "Why do you think 'Pale Blue Eyes' happened on the third album, with Cale out of there? That's a song about Lou's old girlfriend in Syracuse. I said, 'Lou, if I wrote a song like

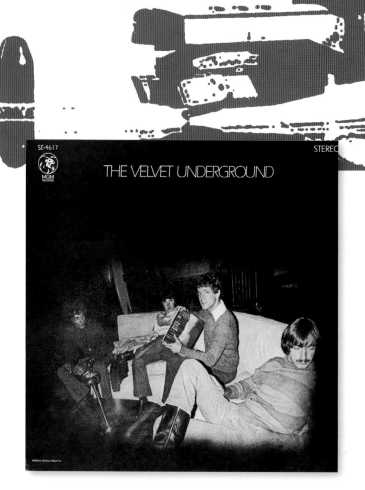

The Velvet Underground, North American stereo issue cover. *Photograph by Billy Name.*

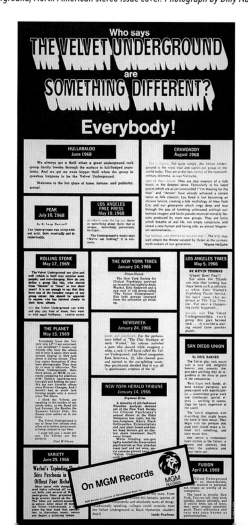

Advertisement, *The Velvet Underground.*

that I wouldn't make you play it.' My position on that album was one of acquiescence."

Except Morrison's "acquiescence" doesn't quite work that way. Where Reed would spend most of his solo career hiring virtuosos such as bassist Fernando Saunders and guitarist Robert Quine to fluff the pillows in the session room, here, he works with his given crew. While it's obvious to note the album contains many of Reed's finest songs—some of which he's spent a career revisiting—*The Velvet Underground* really is Morrison's album. Moe Tucker controls the dynamics of "I'm Set Free" and somehow survives the onslaught of "Beginning To See The Light" without ever turning a drum roll, but it's Morrison's empathetic notes and "acquiescence" that underscore the forlorn alienation of "Candy Says," his frustrated attack that pushes "What Goes On" to its climax, and his reliable, tasteful charm that fills out "That's The Story Of My Life." Without Morrison, this album doesn't get much traction. He may have disliked being called in to service Reed's "Pale Blue Eyes," but it's his stinging guitar notes that accentuate Reed's plaintive delivery and take the song to that rarefied air where the true classics remain. As critic Brian Cullman rightfully wrote, "There were wrong notes and incredibly sloppy solos (check 'Pale Blue Eyes'), but there's not a false note to be found anywhere."

Yet, in the end, it *is* a band effort. Like the ideal socialist commune, each member is used to the best of his or her abilities. Yule adds the harmonies and the melodic complexity that were beyond Reed's scope in "Jesus"—a song that would seem to have been outside of Reed's scope in other ways, too, given his upbringing as a Long Island Jew. (I have trouble believing Lou "found" Jesus any more than he sunk into the junkie trap of "Heroin," though I'm no less moved by his approximations.) Yule's organ throughout "What Goes On" could very well be Cale; Tucker adds the childlike innocence necessary for the closing soft-shoe of the final track "Afterhours," and everyone contributes to the chaos of "The Murder Mystery," which is either another great Velvets trip into *musique concrete* or an overly ambitious literary mess better seen than heard. (I vote for the latter and favor "The Black Angel's Death Song" when I need a freak-out; "The Murder Mystery" was best served as it appeared in the *Paris Review*, as a long poem.)

Reed saw the album as a conceptual whole. "This song would follow this song because this has to do with this and this has to do with that, and this will answer that and then you've got this character who matches this character or offsets this character," he said. His further explanations linking the songs together sound like an after-the-fact

connect-the-dots, a realization or rationalization made to give the album added artistic heft, but it needs none of that. Whether you decide to work through its entire contents or jump in somewhere in the middle, it repays each listen with its singular achievements.

"I've gotten to the point where I like 'pretty' stuff better [than drive and distortion] because you can be more subtle, really say something and sort of soothe, which is what a lot of people seem to need right now," Reed said. "Like I think if you came in after a really hard day at work and played that third album, it might really do you good. A calmative—some people might even call it Muzak—but I think it can function on both that and the intellectual or artistic levels at the same time." ▸

Advertisement and concert promotion, the Boston Tea Party, Boston, Massachusetts, May 29–31, 1969.

Poster, the Boston Tea Party, Boston, Massachusetts, July 11, 1969.

the boston tea party
53 berkeley st
friday july 11

the velvet underground
country funk & quill

tickets krackerjacks george's folly bottega1 headquarters east

─a double odyssey:─
NOVEMBER 5 THRU 10
TAJ MAHAL BLUES BAND
NOVEMBER 6 THRU 10
BIG MAMA THORNTON
NOV. 14 THRU 17 VELVET UNDERGROUND
PLUS SAN FRANCISCO'S COLD BLOOD
NOV. 20 THRU 24 BLACK PEARL AND KALEIDOSCOPE
THANKSGIVING WEEKEND SPECIAL!
NOV. 27 THRU DEC. 1 MOBY GRAPE ALABAMA SHEIKS
WHISKY a GO GO sunset strip
652-4202
NO AGE LIMIT.
JOHANSEN.

Advertisement, Whisky A Go Go, West Hollywood,
California, November 14–17, 1968.

Handbill, Retinal Circus, Vancouver, British Columbia, October 31–November 1, 1968. *Artist: Frank Lewis*

Poster, Stanley Theater, Pittsburgh, Pennsylvania, February 7, 1969. *Artist: Gene King*

To push the release of *The Velvet Underground* in March 1969, MGM mailed out this promotional single. Both sides featured a radio ad for the album, read by Bill "Rosko" Mercer with excerpts from "I'm Set Free," "What Goes On," and "Beginning To See The Light."

Poster, Woodrose Ballroom, Deerfield, Massachusetts, March 21–22, 1969.

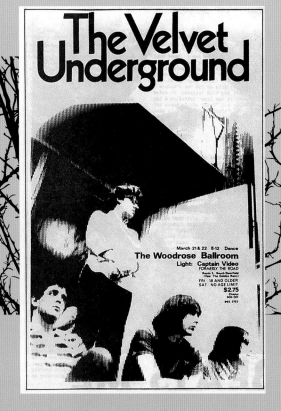

Poster, La Cave, Cleveland, Ohio, March 28–30, 1969.

THE VELVET UNDERGROUND
WILKINSON'S TRICYCLE

MARCH 13, 14, 15
THE BOSTON TEA PARTY
53 BERKELEY ST. 338-7026 LIGHTS BY THE ROAD
Tickets:Krackerjacks, Bottega2, George's Folly WBCN FM SteroRock

Poster, the Boston Tea Party, Boston, Massachusetts, March 13–15, 1969. *Artist: Bob Driscoll*

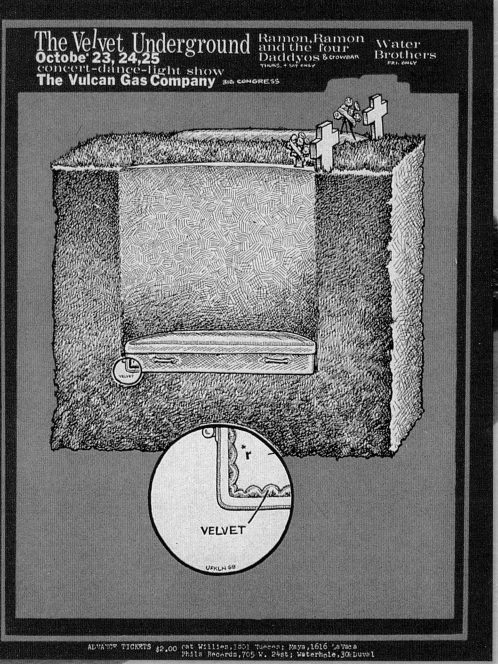

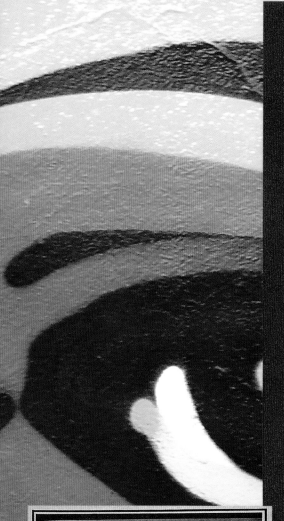

Handbill, End of Cole Ave., Dallas, Texas, October 14–19, 1969.

Handbill, the Vulcan Gas Company, Austin, Texas, October 23–25, 1969. *Artist: Jim Franklin*

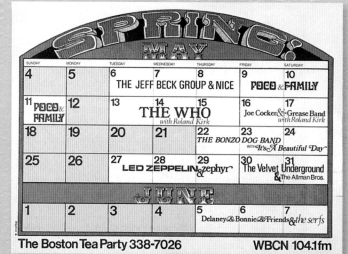

Poster, the Boston Tea Party, Boston, Massachusetts, May 30–31, 1969.
Artist: Engstrom

Toronto Pop Festival 69

Varsity Stadium
June 21/22
1.30 p.m.–11.30 p.m.

SATURDAY, JUNE 21/AFTERNOON

Modern Rock Quartet, Kensington Market, Man,
Eric Andersen, Carla Thomas & The Barkays,
Al Kooper (15 pce. orch.),
The Band "Music from Big Pink"

SATURDAY, JUNE 21/EVENING

S.R.C., Bonzo Dog Band, Elephant's Memory,
Rotary Connection, Johnny Winter,
Velvet Underground, Sly and the Family Stone

SUNDAY, JUNE 22/AFTERNOON

Mother Lode, Stone Soul Children,
Procol Harum, Edwin Starr, Slim Harpo,
Ronnie Hawkins, Chuck Berry, Tiny Tim

SUNDAY, JUNE 22/EVENING

Nucleus, Man, Dr. John "The Night Tripper",
Blood Sweat and Tears (9:00 p.m.),
Charlebois, Steppenwolf

ADVANCE TICKETS
$6 PER DAY –
$10 FOR WEEKEND

ENJOY
Coca-Cola
TRADE MARK REG.

Toronto Pop Festival 1969 Suite 902,
52 Richmond St. West, Toronto 110, Ontario
OR
Attraction Ticket Office
7th Floor, Eaton's College Street (364-6487)
Use your charge.

NOW THRU OCT. 26th

Whisky a go go

CHUCK BERRY
Plus
FIVE MAN ELECTRIC THEATRE

Oct. 29th Thru Nov. 2Nd

THE VELVET UNDERGROUND Plus **The Collectors**

"COMING" THE FLYING BURRITO BROTHERS

652-4202
8901 SUNSET   NO AGE LIMIT   DANCING

[continued from 122]

Whether they were continuing to push on with blind optimism, trying to fulfill the terms of their contract in order to escape, or some combination of the two, the musicians entered the studio again several times between May and October 1969, working with Kellgren at the Record Plant in New York to record songs such as "Foggy Notion," "Andy's Chest" (written after Valerie Solanas shot Warhol in June 1968), the playful "Ferryboat Bill," and the anthemic "I Can't Stand It." Though the proposed follow-up to the third album got as far as being assigned a catalog number, MGM SE-4641, it would never be released, remaining in the realm of legend as "the great lost Velvets album" until the PolyGram corporation finally resurrected the material for two posthumous releases, *VU*, issued in February 1985, and *Another View*, released in September 1986.

The Velvet Underground story was winding down, but the group still had one more significant statement to make.

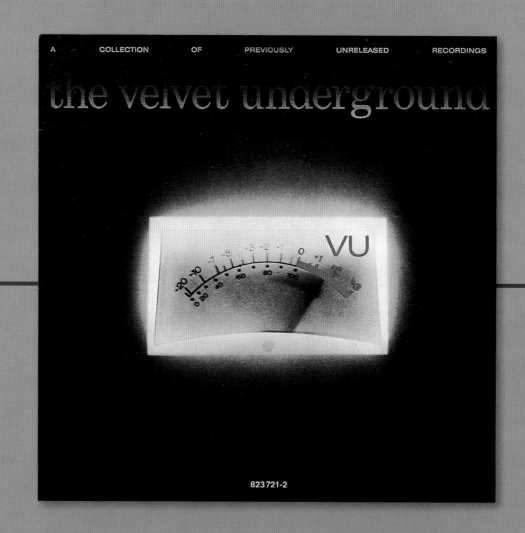

A COLLECTION OF PREVIOUSLY UNRELEASED RECORDINGS

the velvet underground

VU

823721-2

VU, North American issue cover, February 1985. As well as earlier cuts recorded with John Cale, this collection included tracks from the famous "lost" fourth album, catalogued as MGM SE-4641.

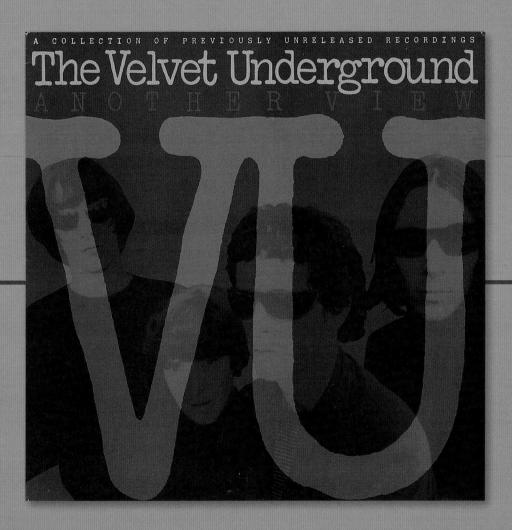

Another View, North American issue cover, September 1986.

LIVE PERFORMANCES

1968–1969

BY OLIVIER LANDEMAINE

February 1, 1968: Aardvark Cinematheque, Chicago. Album release party for *White Light/White Heat* with Warhol put on by Verve two days after the LP was released.

February 24, 1968: The Union, Harvard University, Cambridge, MA

March 15–17, 1968: The Trauma, Philadelphia, PA

March 22–23, 1968: The Boston Tea Party, Boston, MA

April 19–20, 1968: Kinetic Playground, Chicago, IL

April 26–28, 1968: La Cave, Cleveland, OH

May 15, 1968: Merce Cunningham and Dance Company with "Music by the Velvet Underground," Brooklyn Academy of Music, Brooklyn, NY

May 16–18, 1968: The Boston Tea Party, Boston, MA

May 24–25, 1968: Shrine Hall Exposition, Los Angeles, CA

June 7–9, 1968: Avalon Ballroom, San Francisco, CA

June 14–15, 1968: Hippodrome, San Diego, CA

June 27–30, 1968: Retinal Circus, Vancouver, British Columbia, Canada

July 5–6, 1968: Hippodrome, San Diego, CA

July 12–13, 1968: Shrine Auditorium, Los Angeles, CA

July 19–21, 1968: Avalon Ballroom, San Francisco, CA

August 15–17, 1968: The Boston Tea Party, Boston, MA

September 20–21, 1968: Electric Factory and Flea Market, Philadelphia, PA

September 27–28, 1968: The Boston Tea Party, Boston, MA. Last gigs with John Cale.

October 4–6, 1968: La Cave, Cleveland, OH. First dates with Doug Yule.

October 18–20, 1968: Avalon Ballroom, San Francisco, CA

October 23–27, 1968: Whiskey A Go-Go, West Hollywood, CA

October 31–November 3, 1968: Retinal Circus, Vancouver, British Columbia, Canada

November 14–17, 1968: Whiskey A Go-Go, West Hollywood, CA

November 22–24, 1968: Avalon Ballroom, San Francisco, CA

November 28–30, 1968: Avalon Ballroom, San Francisco, CA

December 1, 1968: Music Hall, Cleveland, OH

December 12–14, 1968: The Boston Tea Party, Boston, MA

January 9–11, 1969: The Boston Tea Party, Boston, MA

January 22, 1969: The Boston Tea Party, Boston, MA

January 31–February 2, 1969: La Cave, Cleveland, OH

February 7, 1969: Stanley Theater, Pittsburgh, PA

February 14–15, 1969: Kinetic Playground, Chicago, IL

March 13–15, 1969: The Boston Tea Party, Boston, MA

March 21–22, 1969: Woodrose Ballroom, Deerfield, MA

March 28–30, 1969: La Cave, Cleveland, OH

April 11–13, 1969: Grande Ballroom, Detroit, MI

April 25–27, 1969: Kinetic Playground, Chicago, IL

May 11, 1969: Washington University, St. Louis, MO

May 16–17, 1969: Woodrose Ballroom, Deerfield, MA

May 30–31, 1969: The Boston Tea Party, Boston, MA

June 13–14, 1969: Woodrose Ballroom, Deerfield, MA

June 21, 1969: Toronto Pop Festival 69, Varsity Stadium, Toronto, Ontario, Canada

June 27–28, 1969: The Electric Factory, Philadelphia, PA

July 11, 1969: The Boston Tea Party, Boston, MA

August 2, 1969: Hilltop Festival, Rindge, NH

August 14–16, 1969: The Boston Tea Party, Boston, MA

August 22–23, 1969: Woodrose Ballroom, South Deerfield, MA

Summer 1969: The Electric Factory, Philadelphia, PA

September 1969: The Second Fret, Philadelphia, PA

September 20, 1969: University of Maryland Baltimore County Campus, Catonsville, MD

October 3–4, 1969: Woodrose Ballroom, South Deerfield, MA

October 1969: Music Hall, Cleveland, OH

October 12, 1969: Minneapolis Labor Temple, Minneapolis, MN

October 14–19, 1969: End Of Cole Ave., Dallas, TX

October 23–25, 1969: The Vulcan Gas Company, Austin, TX

October 29–November 2, 1969: Whisky A Go-Go, West Hollywood, CA

October 30–November 1, 1969: The Matrix, San Francisco, CA

November 7–9, 1969: "Family Dog and the Common on the Great Highway," San Francisco, CA

November 12–19, 1969: The Matrix, San Francisco, CA

November 21, 1969: Springer's Hall, Portland, OR

November 22, 1969: The Attic, Eugene, OR

November 23–27, 1969: The Matrix, San Francisco, CA

December 1–3, 1969: The Matrix, San Francisco, CA

Chapter 4

RIDING THE EXPRESS TO *LOADED*

"Lou Reed has always steadfastly maintained that the Velvet Underground were just another Long Island rock 'n' roll band, but in the past, he really couldn't be blamed much if people didn't care to take him seriously. . . . Well, it now turns out that Reed was right all along, and the most surprising thing about the change in the group is that there has been no real change at all."

—Lenny Kaye on *Loaded* in *Rolling Stone*, December 24, 1970

After nearly five years of constant growth, evolution, and struggle, the Velvet Underground entered 1970 with its best prospects since the early days at the Factory in 1966. Dropped by MGM, the band went on to receive one of the ultimate votes of confidence at the time in the form of a new recording contract from Ahmet Ertegun, the revered head of Atlantic Records. But Lou Reed had begun to fight with manager Steve Sesnick, and relations had started to sour between him and Sterling Morrison, who'd resumed his studies at the City College of New York in between commitments to the band. Tucker grew distracted when she became pregnant with her first daughter, born in June, and everyone was exhausted. The band was falling apart even as it began to record some of what would become its best-known songs that April.

The sessions at Atlantic's house studios in New York were the longest and most difficult in the band's history,

"I gave them an album loaded with hits."
—Lou Reed

stretching on for five months under three producers and engineers: Geoffrey Haslam, Shel Kagan, and Adrian Barber. Though she recorded the vocals for "I'm Sticking With You" and added some incidental percussion, Tucker did not play drums on the sessions, and at various times she was replaced by Barber, Doug Yule's brother, Billy, and Long Island session drummer Tommy Castanaro. Backed by Sesnick, who thought he could easily replace the band's founder with its newest member, Doug Yule

The new Velvet Underground members pose for a promotional photograph. From left: Moe Tucker, Sterling Morrison, Doug Yule, and Lou Reed.

time naturally assumed that that was a cloud of dope smoke wafting up from the subway station.

Through the tail end of the *Loaded* sessions, from June through August 1970, the Velvets were booked for a nine-week engagement at Max's Kansas City. This was their triumphant return to live performance in New York, and they played two sets a night while finishing the album during the day. On August 23, Factory regular Brigid Polk, sitting at a table with Gerard Malanga and the young poet Jim Carroll, recorded the performance in the old-school Andy Warhol audio-verité style: The future author of *The Basketball Diaries* can be heard ordering a Pernod and talking about Tuinals in between songs. It turned out to be a memorable night, since at the end of the second set, Reed left the stage, told Sesnick he was quitting the band, and went outside to wait for his parents, who were driving in from Long Island even as their son played his last notes with the Velvets onstage.

Reed was still living at home a few months later when he talked to the band's biggest critical booster on the phone from his father's accounting office. The quotes appeared in a loving eulogy that Lester Bangs penned, entitled "Dead Lie the Velvets Underground, R.I.P., Long Live Lou Reed" and published in *Creem* magazine in May 1971. "I'm not going to make any accusations or blame anybody for what's happened to the Velvets because it's nobody's fault, it's just the way the business is," Reed said. "I just walked out, because we didn't have any money, I didn't want to tour again—I can't get any writing done on tour, and the grind is terrible—and like some other members of the band, I've wondered for a long time if we were *ever* going to be accepted on a scale large enough to make us a 'success.'"

Of course Reed's career did not end with the Velvets—nor, strangely enough, did the Velvets' career end after Reed. 🕶

wound up singing some of the lead vocals, including "New Age," and Reed would grouse about the final mixes and the radio edits made to some of the songs, though his bandmates contend he had much more control over the results than he later claimed.

"I gave them an album loaded with hits, and it was loaded with hits to the point where the rest of the people showed their true colors," Reed has said. Indeed, the best songs on *Loaded*—"Sweet Jane," "Rock & Roll," "New Age," and "Head Held High"—have an instant and undeniable appeal, despite all the amputations during the mixing and the behind-the-scenes computations on the business side of things. Yet while it was the friendliest sound the band had crafted, the group retained just enough of the old outlaw edginess to seem outré: The Velvet Underground forever would be the group that sang "Heroin," and on seeing the album cover, heads at the

Advertisements, Max's Kansas City, New York City, June 24–August 28, 1970.

ATL 10 339

THE VELVET UNDERGROUND
FEATURING
LOU REED

FROM
THE ALBUM
MID 20 049
"LOADED"

SWEET JANE

Rock & Roll

WEA Musik GmbH · Eine Warner Communications Gesellschaft · Made in Germany

"Sweet Jane"/"Rock & Roll," German single, 1970.

First New York Appearance In 3 Years!

THE VELVET UNDERGROUND

ATLANTIC RECORDING ARTISTS

Wednesday-Sunday JUNE 24-28
Wednesday-Sunday JULY 1-5
11 PM & 1 AM

UPSTAIRS AT
MAX'S KANSAS CITY
213 Park Ave. South (At 17th St.) 777-7870

MAKE YOUR DREAM KITCHEN COME TRUE

2400 111 (also available on Musicassette)
Loaded.

2315 056
The Velvet Underground & Nico.

2353 022
The Velvet Underground.

2353 024
White Light/White Heat.

2683 006 (double album)
Andy Warhol's Velvet Underground featuring Nico.

MARKETED BY POLYDOR

MGM

MARKETED BY POLYDOR

With the launch of *Loaded*, MGM sought to re-promote the band's back catalog.

'Le Soupçon' by David Gourd (the well-known fraud).

THE VELVET UNDERGROUND

"Loaded With Hits"
Singing a Swan Song on *Loaded*
(Atlantic Records, 1970)

By Garth Cartwright

When the Velvet Underground began work on their fourth album in April 1970, all omens appeared positive: Newly signed to hit-making, ground-breaking Atlantic Records after three years on Verve (a label better known for its jazz releases), bandleader Lou Reed was writing catchy, radio-friendly songs. Atlantic boss Ahmet Ertegun had told Reed he wanted an album "loaded with hits," unintentionally christening the recording sessions. Yet by the time *Loaded* was released, Reed had quit the band, effectively sabotaging any commercial momentum.

Loaded proved to be the Velvet Underground's swan song, and it stands as an album that divides the band's fans: Detractors complain that it is too commercial, that four of the ten vocals are by bassist Doug Yule, that Maureen Tucker was absent due to maternity leave (drums were played by several people, including Yule, engineer Adrian Barber, session musician Tommy Castanaro, and Yule's teenage brother Billy), and Reed is even criticized for his ragged voice and tamed lyrics. Diehard John Cale–era Velvets fans have been known to dismiss *Loaded* as a "sellout," to which band members must have muttered, "If only!" Guitarist Sterling Morrison suggested that it "showed we could have, all along, made truly commercial-sounding records. We usually opted not to . . . but people would wonder, 'Could they do it if they had to?' The answer was, 'Yes, we could.' And we did."

A pity, then, that so few got to enjoy *Loaded* when it was released in September 1970. But almost four decades later, it is held in the same high esteem as the three previous Velvets albums.

With *Loaded*, Reed was intent on becoming something more than a cult figure, one admired only by Manhattan's demimonde and critics. Lyrically and musically, the album often finds Reed reflecting on the music that initially shaped his love of pop. This sense of the bandleader shuffling through his back pages means *Loaded* is the least thematically coherent Velvets album: Reed tries on (and generally fits) a variety of popular musical formats. Yet the punk in him still surfaces on several occasions to stop things from getting too smooth.

The album opener "Who Loves The Sun" is a great "name the band" tease as, with its West Coast harmonies, Yule's plangent tenor vocal, and winsome flavor, it sounds unlike any previous Velvet Underground recording.

Loaded, North American issue cover.

Loaded two-CD "Fully Loaded Edition," 1997.

"Sweet Jane" finds Reed ad-libbing a loose, hip narrative over a swinging guitar riff, and it's a song bursting with New York's arrogant energies. And yet on the original release, Reed's song lost the bridge due to postproduction politics and hack surgery; the bridge was finally added back decades later in restored versions of the album. Still, "Sweet Jane" has become a standard, with several successful cover versions, and it remains a staple in Reed's live performances.

Almost as good is "Rock & Roll," Reed's tribute to how pop radio saved his alienated adolescent self: "'Rock & Roll' is about me," he once noted. "If I hadn't heard rock 'n' roll on the radio, I would have had no idea there was life on this planet. Which would have been devastating—to think that everything, everywhere was like it was where I come from. That would have been profoundly discouraging. Movies didn't do it for me. TV didn't do it for me. It was the radio that did it."

"Cool It Down" keeps things very New York, with its hipster lingo and bluesy feel recalling both Reed's earlier "I'm Waiting For The Man" and Bob Dylan circa *Blonde On Blonde*. Reed was advised by Ertegun to avoid controversial subject matter on *Loaded*, and when one contrasts the versions of "New Age" found on this album and *1969: The Velvet Underground Live*, it's apparent that Reed took his advice, rewriting the lyrics and dropping the line "You know that it's my fancy to make it with Franky and Sue Ann" for a more innocent alternative. Yule's fragile tenor suits the reflective lyric of "You're over the hill right now/ And you're looking for love," but oddly, the song ends with the chanted chorus of "It's the beginning of a new age," which sabotages its gentle, beatific nature.

Side Two opens with "Head Held High," a storming slice of garage-punk nonsense that could have been written and recorded by Reed's pre-Velvets band, the Primitives. Reed's vocal is ragged from the Velvets' nine-week

residency at a Manhattan music venue—concerts that later gave birth to the very primitive live album, *Live at Max's Kansas City*.

"Lonesome Cowboy Bill" finds Reed ironically referencing country music, thereby creating a proto-alt-country tune. Reed and Morrison scratch out a Rolling Stones–style riff, while Reed adds a splash of honky-tonk piano. Yet this was a bit of quaint, old-timey Americana only on the surface: the song was a tongue-in-cheek hootenanny in honor of literary revolutionary William S. Burroughs, a rebellious antigodfather to the VU.

"I Found A Reason" harks back to Reed's doo-wop roots with the Shades. Superb harmonies accompany Yule's deadpan monologue, which deconstructs teenage romance and the American belief that things always improve.

"Train Round The Bend" finds the Velvets' garage-band groove cranked up high with Yule's repetitive keyboard riff chugging brilliantly throughout. Reed's lyric goes against the then-fashionable concept of "getting it together in the country" as he moans how nothing that he plants seems to grow and he wants to get back to the city. Here the members of the Velvet Underground are once again snarling punks who hate the hippies.

The album closer "Oh! Sweet Nuthin'" is another slice of country rock that recalls the music then being made by the Flying Burrito Brothers. Yule's yearning vocal lends the song an elegiac quality that ends both the album and the Velvets' recording career, while Reed's lyric suggests exhaustion both with his band and with life in general. Having quit the Velvets in August while *Loaded* was in postproduction, supposedly due to conflicts with Yule, Reed left New York City to live with his parents in the suburbs of Long Island.

The 1970s would soon find the Velvet Underground's legacy embraced and celebrated internationally; *Loaded* remains a remarkable signpost for many of the band's followers as they navigate from the group's noisy beginnings to simpler, more evocative possibilities. 🕶

Advertisement, *Loaded.*

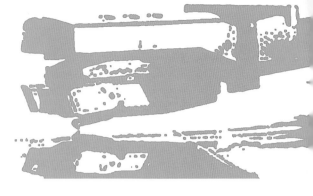

Live Velvets

1969: Velvet Underground Live with Lou Reed (Mercury, 1974)

By Greg Kot

The gatefold double album was as much a part of the 1970s as shag rugs and polyester suits. Many had fold-out covers depicting rock stars striking rock-star poses, most notably the fair-haired Peter Frampton. A far less celebrated band, the Velvet Underground, also released a double album during that era with slightly more provocative gatefold art: the semi-exposed buttocks of a hot-pants-wearing hooker in stiletto heels. Which begs the question: Who's the bigger whore?

Cheap-thrills sensationalism aside, *1969: Velvet Underground Live with Lou Reed* did have a few things in common with more famous seventies franchises such as *Frampton Comes Alive*, Bob Seger's *Live Bullet*, and *Cheap Trick at Budokan*: It essentially was a live, career-spanning greatest-hits set designed to pimp a long-ignored band/artist to a new audience. It didn't quite achieve a Frampton-esque level of sales, but *1969 Live* did its job well when it was released in 1974: It presented a mix of the defunct band's best songs from its studio albums, plus a handful of illuminating rarities that either were unreleased or issued in inferior versions on Reed solo albums. For many who stumbled across it, *1969 Live* was their first exposure to the shadowy quartet, and its timing couldn't have been more apt: The cultural and musical landmines the Velvets left behind were about to erupt.

The band had faded away in 1970, unmourned and virtually unheard outside of a devoted cult. Its four brilliant studio albums would soon be available only as cut-outs in record-store bargain bins—if you could find them at all. But by the time *1969 Live* came out, the Velvets' reputation was slowly expanding, in part because of the notoriety accruing around Reed and his flamboyant solo career: He'd had his first and only Top 40 hit in 1973 with "Walk On The Wild Side," and the Velvets were becoming a touchstone for the nascent punk movement, inspiring a new wave of bands from New York to London etched in the Velvet verities of minimalism, mayhem, and street poetry.

The man responsible for bringing the *1969 Live* tapes to the public was Paul Nelson, an astute music critic who briefly worked as a talent scout at Mercury Records during the early seventies. (He signed the New York Dolls.) Nelson had tracked down eight hours of relatively high-quality recordings of Velvets performances in San Francisco and Dallas, then winnowed them down to seventeen tracks. Rocker Elliott Murphy penned liner notes that passionately rhapsodized about the Velvets' place in rock history. (To sum up: They were really good but ahead of their time.)

As good as the Velvet Underground was in the studio—and its four studio albums are virtually a blueprint for (you name it) punk, postpunk, art-punk, alternative rock, and on, and on—it was even better in concert. Countless bootlegs make the case, though shockingly few authorized releases do. *The Velvet Underground Live at Max's Kansas City* was the first to surface in 1972; it documents a band on its last legs. Drummer Maureen Tucker was off on maternity leave, replaced by Billy Yule. In retrospect, it's sacrilege to think that an "official" Velvets album was released with anyone but Tucker on drums, but such was the state of the VU in 1970, when *Max's Kansas City* was recorded on the very night that Reed quit the band and retreated to his parents' home on Long Island. Partly as a result, the music sounds as if it is being played by a somewhat distracted Velvets cover band.

Two decades later, the original band—Reed, Tucker, John Cale, and Sterling Morrison—gathered for a brief, ill-fated reunion and a tour of Europe. The 1993 double CD *Live MCMXCIII* portrayed a tense power struggle between Reed and Cale, with the music caught in the middle: It's a recital of past glories rather than an affirmation of the quartet's continuing relevance.

Far better is *The Velvet Underground Bootleg Series Volume 1: The Quine Tapes*. Released in 2001, it presents three discs of recordings made by Velvets groupie and future avant-punk guitarist extraordinaire Robert Quine. It documents the same tour as *1969 Live*, when the band was still operating at a high level, and the performances are terrific, if a bit lacking in sonic fidelity.

For a relatively concise overview of the Velvets on stage, *1969 Live* remains the gold standard. The quartet was once again stable after a tumultuous period that saw the ouster of Cale and the introduction of Doug Yule to play bass and keyboards alongside Reed, Morrison, and Tucker. It was this lineup that recorded the eponymous studio album released earlier in 1969, and that third

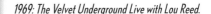
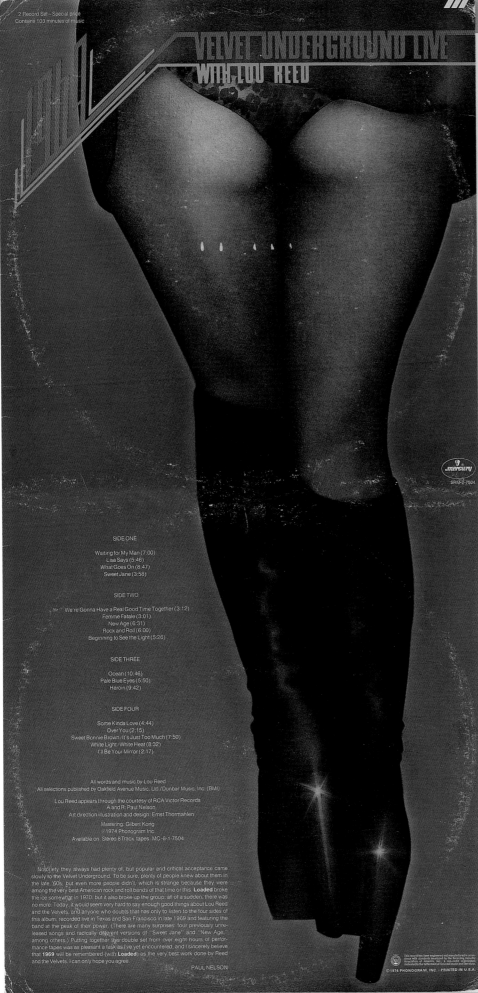

Velvets album presented the band in a new light: Here was a more relaxed, intimate ensemble that focused on delivering Reed's bittersweet melodies with a minimum of fuss.

Reed went on a songwriting roll after the third album's release, crafting dozens of songs and recording a number of them with the band for a new studio album, which soon became a casualty of the Velvets' long-running label problems. When the quartet hit the road in the fall of 1969, it was in excellent form. The push–pull between Reed and Cale that electrified the band's early incarnation had given way to a more defined hierarchy. Reed's voice and rhythm guitar were now clearly driving everything, but though the music was less overtly violent and sensational, it was no less powerful. Indeed, for those who had heard about the band's notorious reputation as sixties troublemakers, the house band for Andy Warhol's traveling Exploding Plastic Inevitable and its whip-wielding go-go dancers, *1969 Live* might have come as a surprise. The cover art promised more seedy thrills, but the music is relaxed yet intense, performed by a well-rehearsed unit completely in sync with the entrancing power of the songs.

Consider the amphetamine blur of "White Light/White Heat," with its short-circuiting guitars, and the almost comical rituals described in "I'm Waiting For The Man." These songs convey a matter-of-fact understanding of drugs and the desperation that comes with them, yet their level of lyrical detail and the performances themselves pulse with pulpy, blood-pumping energy. In other moments, Reed pays tribute to his heroes and influences. "Over You" is the kind of lilting, melancholy love song that Buddy Holly might have written; "Sweet Bonnie Brown/It's Just Too Much" motors along like a fifties Chess Records single by Chuck Berry; and "We're Gonna Have A Real Good Time Together" ratchets up rockabilly with a corrosive, overdriven "solo" that is pure rhythm. "Awww, watch me now," Reed demands before making his guitar sound like a roaring subway train.

On "What Goes On," Reed and Morrison do their best Bo-Diddley-in-overdrive on guitars while Tucker stays on top of the beat with the doggedness of a pit bull. Yule throws some roller-rink organ over the top, and it feels like it could just go on and on—and nearly does, for nine glorious minutes.

Reed also road-tests a trio of pop anthems that would end up on the next Velvets album, *Loaded*, to be recorded the following year. "Sweet Jane" is still a work in progress as heard on *1969 Live*, with considerably different lyrics and a more muted, contemplative tune. It's absolutely lovely, the sublime melody lifted by Yule's complementary bass line. "New Age," also with different lyrics than would end up on *Loaded*, closes with a Wembley-size chorus. "Rock & Roll" celebrates everything great embodied by its title: rhythm, joy, and more cowbell. "And it was alriiiiiight," Reed exults.

That joy counters Elliott Murphy's assertion that the Velvets "wrote and played sad music." They did, but only in that life is sometimes sad. Their songs speak to a broader experience, and at its core is a respect for human dignity that comes through more loudly and clearly in the Velvets' music because Reed chose to write about characters who normally aren't treated with much respect by mainstream society. If the Velvets had only been about the wild-side encounters suggested by the *1969 Live* album cover, they would've been a footnote a long time ago.

The tone is set by Reed's opening monologue: "We saw your Cowboys today and they never let Philadelphia have the ball for a minute," he tells an audience in Dallas. "It was 42-7 by the half; it was ridiculous. You should give other people just a little chance—in football, anyway."

Empathy isn't a word normally associated with Reed or his music, but it underlines his greatest work. "Heroin," easily one of the most chilling songs in rock history, is given a stunning, nearly ten-minute treatment on *1969 Live*. (The two-volume CD reissue offers two nearly identical versions.) Tucker traces the story line like a jazz percussionist, and her tympani-style drumming with mallets gives the song an orchestral dimension. Reed's guitar tones evoke a bell, then a hammer. The story moves from the craving ("It's my life and it's my wife"), to the rush, to the nodding-off aftermath. Smack is the junkie's anodyne, temporarily blotting out a universe full of death and lies ("All the politicians making crazy sounds, and all the dead bodies piled up in mounds"). The song doesn't condemn or condone the decision to shoot up but places it in a context where it becomes understandable.

"Heroin" is book-ended in scope and intent by another epic song, the ten-minute "Ocean." Just as the addict vows to "nullify my life," "Ocean" ends in self-inflicted death. But, as always with Reed's best songs, there's much more to the story, and he and the band take their time giving it shape and color. Tucker's cymbals wash and wane, and the guitars suggest surf music slowed way down. The waves of sound are at first soothing, then consuming, until they finally swallow everything, including the song's protagonist. Madness, like the waves, doesn't come all at once.

"Ocean" also feels like the band's epitaph. The disintegration of the Velvets would begin a few months later, and Reed would leave in the middle of the recording sessions for *Loaded*. But they had one great round of concerts in them before they were pulled under, and *1969 Live* captures the moment when they were riding the crest of the wave for the last time. 🕶

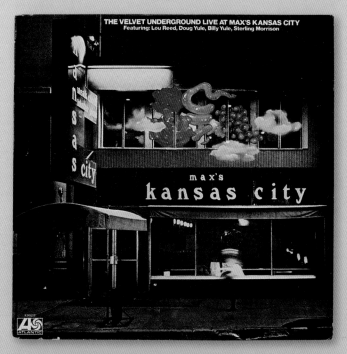

The Velvet Underground Live at Max's Kansas City.

LIVE PERFORMANCES 1970

BY OLIVIER LANDEMAINE

Late December 1969–January 3, 1970: The Second Fret, Philadelphia, PA

January 9, 1970: Paramount Theater, Springfield, MA

January 15 & 21, 1970: The Quiet Knight, Chicago, IL

February 1970: Head Quarters, Reading, PA

February 19–22, 1970: The Main Point, Bryn Mawr, PA

February 28, 1970: Pal Joey's, Chicago, IL

April 17, 1970: Paramount Theater, Springfield, MA

May 8–10, 1970: The Second Fret, Philadelphia, PA

May 22–June 7, 1970: The Unicorn, Boston, MA

Summer 1970: Central Park, New York City

June 24–August 28, 1970: The Max's Kansas City, New York City

November 19–22, 1970: The Main Point, Bryn Mawr, PA. New lineup without Reed.

Chapter 5

WHAT BECOMES A LEGEND MOST? (WELL BABY TONIGHT IT'S YOU)

"What it comes down to for me—as a Velvets fan, a lover of rock-and-roll, a New Yorker, an aesthete, a punk, a sinner, a sometime seeker of enlightenment (and love) (and sex)—is this: I believe that we are all, openly or secretly, struggling against one or another kind of nihilism. I believe that body and spirit are not really separate, though it often seems that way. I believe that redemption is never impossible and always equivocal. But I guess that I just don't know."

—Ellen Willis

Though the remaining members of the Velvet Underground no doubt were stunned by Lou Reed's departure, the band's momentum carried them several years into the next decade. "[Manager Steve] Sesnick was the one who said 'Lou won't be here,'" Doug Yule recalled in his interview with *Perfect Sound Forever*. "We just kept going; what else could you do really?"

Yule, Maureen Tucker, Sterling Morrison, and a new recruit, Yule's friend Walter Powers, continued to tour as the Velvet Underground, capitalizing on the generally positive reception that greeted *Loaded* after its release in September 1970. Morrison left the next year and was replaced by another of Yule's old Boston bandmates, Willie "Loco" Alexander; after that, Tucker began to drift

in and out of the picture. In time, Sesnick arranged a deal for another studio album with Polydor in the United Kingdom, and Yule recorded it on his own in London in the fall of 1972, playing many of the instruments himself, with the exception of drums by Deep Purple's Ian Paice—always the jazziest of heavy-metal drummers, and the stylistic opposite of Tucker—and some unnamed studio musicians on sax and female backing vocals.

By the time the aptly named *Squeeze* was released in February 1973, Yule had given up on the final version of the band, which contained none of the original members, after Sesnick slithered away and left the group stranded in the midst of a botched European tour. Never issued in the United States, the final Velvet

The Velvet Underground photographed in London during their reunion tour, May 1993. From left: Moe Tucker, Sterling Morrison, Lou Reed, and John Cale. *Steve Double/Retna*

Squeeze, the 1973 album from Doug Yule's "Velveteen Underground," released only in Great Britain.

Underground studio album remains a curious footnote. Musically, Yule followed the pop-rock direction of some of the lesser songs on *Loaded*—"Lonesome Cowboy Bill" and "Train Round The Bend"—while lyrically, he adapted one of Reed's favorite motifs, the character portrait à la "Candy Says," though with much less distinguished results on generic tunes such as "Little Jack," "Dopey Joe," "Jack & Jane," and "Louise."

"Someone said to me, 'You can go into a studio and you can record your songs.' And I thought, 'Great, every songwriter's dream,'" Yule said. "It's kind of a nice memory for me and kind of an embarrassment at the same time. . . . A lot of that stuff is about Lou; some of it is about Maureen." Though he has been vilified in some quarters as a mercenary who wrung the last dime out of the Velvet Underground name, it's interesting to note that Reed did not seem to hold any animosity toward him at first, and Yule contributed to a track on Reed's 1974 solo album *Sally Can't Dance*, as well as touring with the band that supported that release.

On the other hand, during their reunion in the early 1990s, Reed and John Cale both vetoed the idea of Yule participating when Morrison suggested it—he had always disliked playing bass when Cale moved to organ or viola—and Yule was excluded when the band was inducted into the Rock and Roll Hall of Fame in 1996.

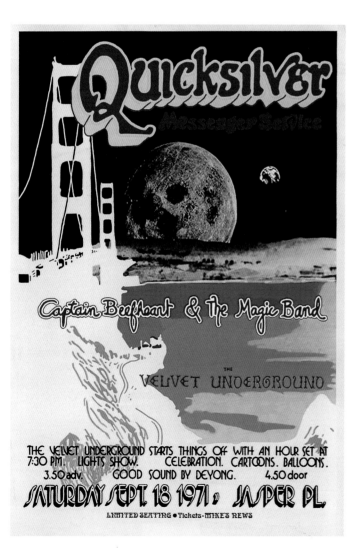

Handbill and poster, "Velveteen Underground" concerts, 1971.

Of course the two driving forces of the early Velvet Underground both have had long solo careers, though in almost all of their guises they've usually included Velvets songs in concert, and the shadow of the band looms large over everything else they've accomplished.

Throughout the 1970s Reed shifted from style to style, adopting one strange persona after another. His self-titled 1972 debut had some of the trappings of progressive rock, though several of the songs dated back to the Velvets, and *Transformer* (1972) yielded a hit with "Walk On The Wild Side," a simplified version of the character studies he'd done of people at the Factory. *Sally Can't Dance* (1974) and *Coney Island Baby* (1976) flirted with mainstream pop, but in between came the nearly unlistenable white-noise assault of the infamous *Metal Machine Music* (1975)—"Sister Ray" taken to the extreme with all semblance of melody removed. Meanwhile, the title track of *Street Hassle* (1978) told a similar story to the one in that Velvets epic, attempting a punk operetta complete with strings.

With tracks such as "Disco Mystic," "I Want To Boogie With You," and "The Power Of Positive Drinking," most of *The Bells* (1979) and *Growing Up in Public* (1980) is best forgotten, but with *The Blue Mask* (1982) and *Legendary Hearts* (1983), Reed once again found a measure of the ideal creative collaboration he'd had with the Velvets. Guitarist Robert Quine was a veteran of Richard Hell and the Voidoids and a VU superfan who later lovingly compiled *The Velvet Underground Bootleg Series Volume 1: The Quine Tapes*, a three-disc box set released by Polydor in 2001. He complemented Reed by combining a measure of some of the best aspects of Cale and Morrison, searing noise and solid rhythm, but the pairing did not last.

On *New York* (1989), a loving homage to the city that has always been such a large part of his work, Reed seemed to arrive at his final incarnation as a distinguished elder statesman and literary professor of rock. This is the persona that dominates *Magic and Loss*, his 1992 contemplation of death and dying; *Ecstasy*, his 2000 homage to love and marriage; *The Raven*, his 2003 musical reworking of Edgar Allan Poe, and *Berlin: Live at St. Ann's Warehouse*, his 2008 resurrection of his dense, depressing, but brilliant 1974 album *Berlin*. Yet fans still can never be certain of when Reed will throw an unexpected curve ball, and it boggles the mind to think that the same artist who gave us *Metal Machine Music* also produced *Hudson River Wind Meditations*, a 2007 set of ambient music written to accompany his tai chi workouts.

[continued on 156]

Miscellany of Lou Reed solo LPs.

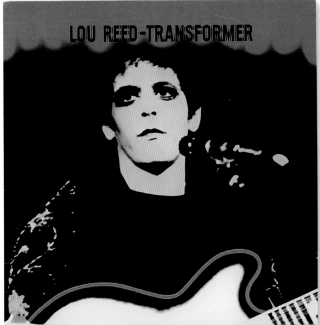

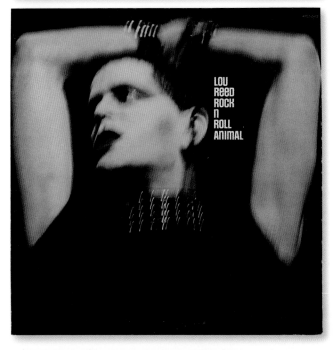

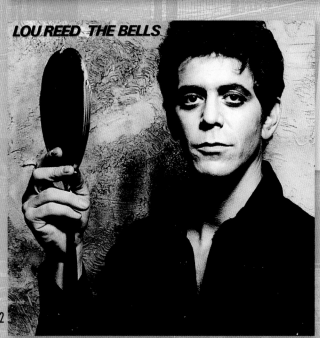

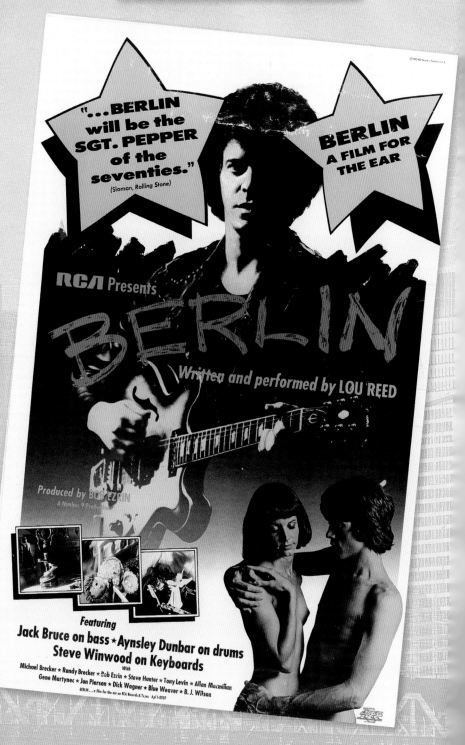

Miscellany of Lou Reed solo LPs.

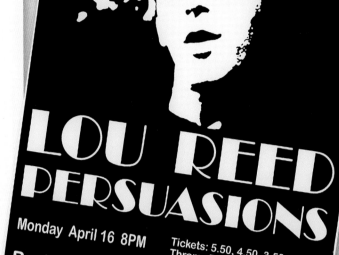

Posters, Lou Reed solo concerts.

LOU REED'S BERLIN

photo: Amy-Beth McNeely

"Berlin is the wonder, a devastating reminder of what rock can be"
The Independent ★ ★ ★ ★

"One of the most chilling but absorbing shows in rock history"
The Guardian ★ ★ ★ ★

"The performance is gripping. This is why he is still one of rock's greats"
The Sunday Times ★ ★ ★ ★

"Reed and his 25-piece band featuring an angelic choir and mini-orchestra resolutely deliver"
The Daily Telegraph ★ ★ ★ ★

PERFORMED BY LOU REED WITH BAND, CHOIR, STRINGS AND HORNS
MUSIC PRODUCERS **BOB EZRIN** AND **HAL WILLNER**
DIRECTED AND DESIGNED BY **JULIAN SCHNABEL**

26 JUNE 2008
NOTTINGHAM ROYAL CENTRE
0870 121 0123

www.AEGlive.co.uk / Ticketmaster 08444 775 775 / See Tickets 0870 405 0448 / Ticketline 0870 444 5556
For hospitality packages call 0800 288 9822

An AEG Live presentation in association with Primary Talent International

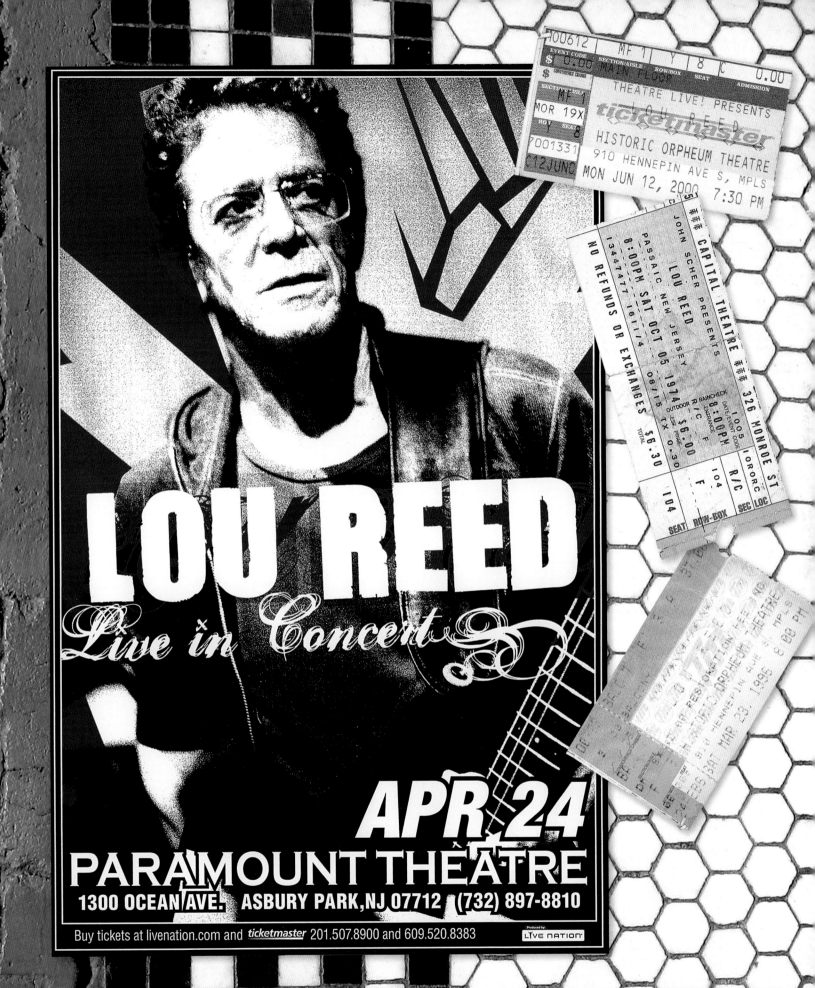

[continued from 151]

Every bit as rewarding and slightly more consistent in its stylistic detours, Cale's solo canon ranges from early art-rock albums such as *The Academy in Peril* (1972) and *Paris 1919* (1973) to the furious punk explosion of *Fear* (1974), and from his own version of Reed's "collaboration" with Poe—*Words for the Dying*, a 1989 album largely built upon the poems of Dylan Thomas—to recent electronic forays such as *HoboSapiens* (2003) and *blackAcetate* (2005). While Reed is considered the songwriting genius of the Velvets and Cale is the master musician, the best cases for the depth and rewarding complexity of the latter's song craft are the 1992 live album *Fragments of a Rainy Season* and the 1994 compilation *Seducing Down the Door*— "two sides of one coin," as Cale wrote. "They're good companion pieces because you see both sides of how

the songs are performed, how they've stood up over time and how they were originally."

Cale also played a big role in the best solo albums by Nico, *The Marble Index* (1969) and *Desertshore* (1970), both gorgeous if at times relentlessly dark and depressing epics. A sad soul who battled heroin addiction for much of her life, Nico spent many of her years after the Velvets eking out a meager living as a cult heroine, a tale traced with humor and warmth in *Songs They Never Play on the Radio*, a 1999 book written by one of her touring musicians, James Young. As a formative influence on the Gothic sound, style, and ambience, Nico tops even Siouxsie Sioux as the witchiest woman in rock history. Ironically, she died on a sunny day in Ibiza in July 1988 after suffering a minor heart attack while bicycling, hitting her head, and incurring a severe cerebral hemorrhage.

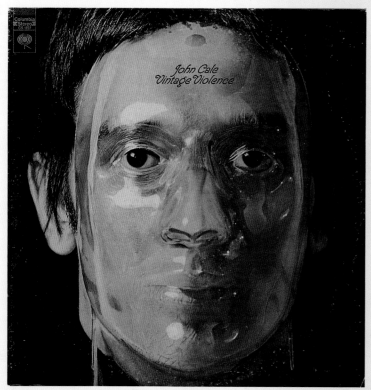

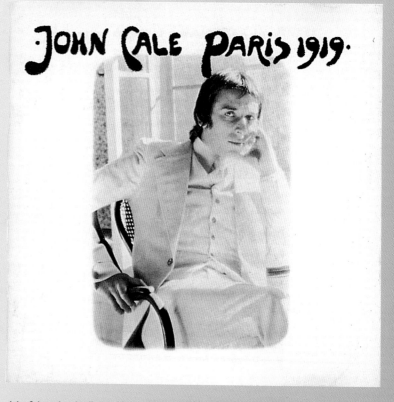

John Cale early solo albums, *Vintage Violence* (1970) and *Paris 1919* (1973).

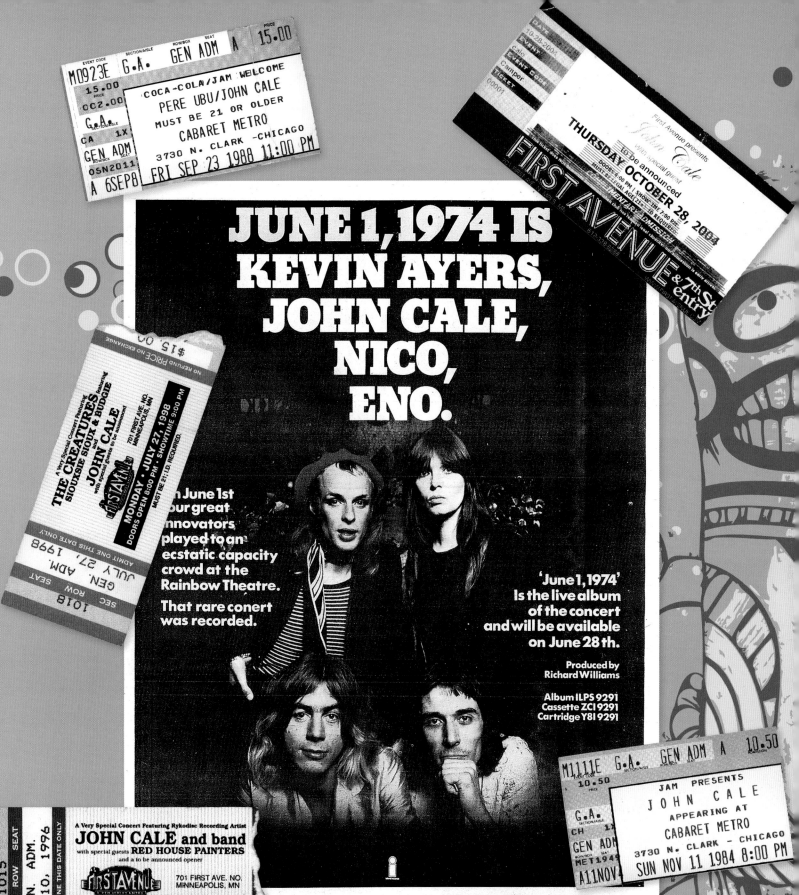

JUNE 1, 1974 IS KEVIN AYERS, JOHN CALE, NICO, ENO.

On June 1st four great innovators played to an ecstatic capacity crowd at the Rainbow Theatre.

That rare concert was recorded.

'June 1, 1974' Is the live album of the concert and will be available on June 28th.

Produced by Richard Williams

Album ILPS 9291
Cassette ZCI 9291
Cartridge Y8I 9291

Advertisement, *June 1, 1974*, featuring John Cale and Nico with Brian Eno and Kevin Ayers.

EVENT CODE M0923E G·A· GEN ADM A PRICE 15.00
COCA-COLA/JAM WELCOME
PERE UBU/JOHN CALE
MUST BE 21 OR OLDER
CABARET METRO
3730 N. CLARK - CHICAGO
FRI SEP 23 1988 11:00 PM

First Avenue presents
John Cale
with special guest
to be announced
THURSDAY OCTOBER 28, 2004
FIRST AVENUE & 7th St entry

A Very Special Concert Featuring
THE CREATURES featuring
SIOUXSIE SIOUX & BUDGIE
and
JOHN CALE
with special guests to be announced
MONDAY · JULY 27, 1998
DOORS OPEN 8:00 PM · SHOWTIME 9:00 PM
701 FIRST AVE. NO. MINNEAPOLIS, MN
MUST BE 21. I.D. REQUIRED.
$15.00
NO REFUND PRICE NO EXCHANGE

A Very Special Concert Featuring Rykodisc Recording Artist
JOHN CALE and band
with special guests RED HOUSE PAINTERS
and a to be announced opener
First Avenue
701 FIRST AVE. NO.
MINNEAPOLIS, MN
THURSDAY · OCTOBER 10, 1996
DOORS OPEN 8:00 PM · SHOWTIME 9:00 PM
MUST BE LEGAL AGE. I.D. REQUIRED.

EVENT CODE M1111E G·A· GEN ADM A 10.50
JAM PRESENTS
JOHN CALE
APPEARING AT
CABARET METRO
3730 N. CLARK - CHICAGO
SUN NOV 11 1984 8:00 PM

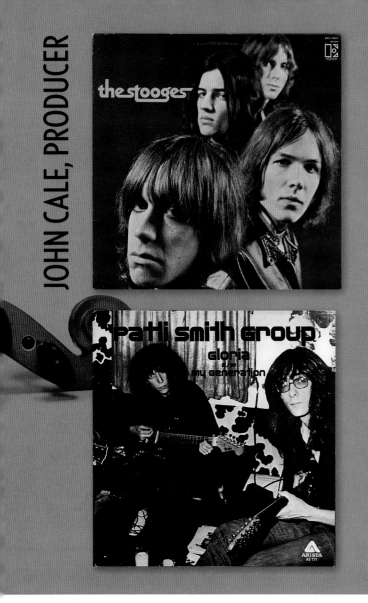

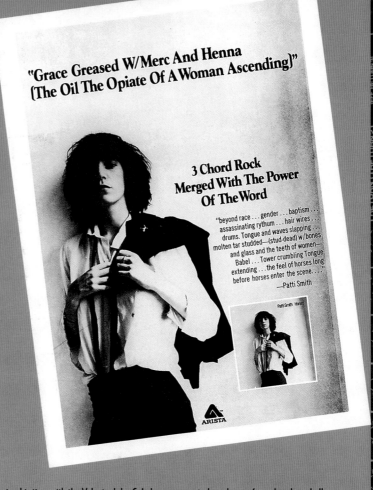

"Grace Greased W/Merc And Henna
(The Oil The Opiate Of A Woman Ascending)"

3 Chord Rock
Merged With The Power
Of The Word

"beyond race . . . gender . . . baptism . . .
assassinating rythum . . . hair wires . . .
drums. Tongue and waves slapping . . .
molten tar studded—(stud-dead) w/bones
and glass and the teeth of women . . .
Babel . . . Tower crumbling Tongue
extending . . . the feel of horses long
before horses enter the scene. . . ."
—Patti Smith

Following his time with the Velvets, John Cale became a noted producer of new bands and albums, starting with the Stooges debut in 1969. He contributed bass to the Patti Smith Group's single "Gloria" and produced her first LP, *Horses* (1975). Along with producing Jonathan Richman and the Modern Lovers' debut in 1976, he oversaw recordings by Nico, Siouxsie and the Banshees, and Alejandro Escovedo among others.

Much less dark and destructive, Tucker also has enjoyed a Velvets afterlife as a cult heroine, periodically taking a break from raising her four children to record simple, charming, and not surprisingly drum-heavy indie-rock excursions such as *Playin' Possum* (1981), *Life in Exile After Abdication* (1989), *Dogs Under Stress* (1994), and *Moe Rocks Terrastock* (2002), which features contributions from Yule.

As for Morrison, the third original band member referred to in the group's initial publishing company Three Prong Music, not long after leaving the Velvets he moved to Texas to pursue a life in academia. He eventually earned a doctorate in medieval studies, in between time spent piloting tugboats in the Houston Ship Channel. (The song "Tugboat" by Velvets acolytes Galaxie 500 is thought to be a tribute to him.) Sometimes reticent to revisit his rock 'n' roll past, he did pick up his guitar from time to time to play in Austin's vibrant music scene, tour with Tucker's band, or make the odd guest

appearance on a recording such as the 1994 Luna album *Bewitched*.

Morrison's most significant return to the spotlight came during the brief Velvets reunion tour in the summer of 1993. Two years later, on August 30, 1995, he died of non-Hodgkin's lymphoma at his home in Poughkeepsie, New York. He was fifty-three.

Appropriately enough, the roots of the Velvets' reunion can be traced back to their original sponsor, Andy Warhol, who died on February 22, 1987, from a cardiac arrhythmia while recuperating from gallbladder surgery. In early 1989 Reed and Cale came together to pay tribute to Warhol with a set of new songs that they co-wrote and performed at St. Anne's Church in Brooklyn; several months later they played the set again at the Brooklyn Academy of Music and recorded those shows for a live album. Though Cale was angry that Reed took control of the mix, the music was poignant and powerful, and *Songs for Drella* was released in April 1990. In June, Reed and Cale were

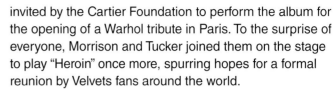

Maureen Tucker's debut LP, *Playin' Possum*, 1981.

Maureen Tucker miscellaneous singles and albums.

invited by the Cartier Foundation to perform the album for the opening of a Warhol tribute in Paris. To the surprise of everyone, Morrison and Tucker joined them on the stage to play "Heroin" once more, spurring hopes for a formal reunion by Velvets fans around the world.

Considerable negotiating led to the 1993 tour documented on *Live MCMXCIII*. Most of the band's live sets were compOsed of highlights from the 1960s, and the album only includes two new songs, neither of which is extraordinary. "Velvet Nursery Rhyme" attempts to make a self-deprecating comment on the reunion but winds up being campy and mawkish ("We're the Velvet Underground and we have come to play/It's been twenty-eight years since we've been here to the day. . . . Now you got here John and me, we want no part of this/That's because we think it is real pretentious shit."). Holding out the promise of an eventual lift-off, "Coyote" is all build-up with no delivery, and though the lyrics don't reference it, it's hard not to think of the parable of the coyote chewing off its own leg to escape the trap.

By the time *Live MCMXCIII* was released in October 1993 the reunion was over. All of the old tensions between the musicians quickly returned—first and foremost Reed's desire for control clashing with Cale's urge toward chaos—and the Velvets broke up again and—given Morrison's death—most likely for good.

For a band that always had been about living in the moment while forging a sound that bravely pointed toward the future, the idea of revisiting the past seemed incongruous anyway, and there can be no better celebration of the Velvet Underground's legacy than losing oneself in the glorious noise of its first four studio albums and the best of the many live recordings from the periods in between. The music remains as vital, timeless, and infinitely rich as the day it was made, offering listeners bottomless depths to plumb, and in the end, this may be the Velvets' biggest contribution: proving that rock 'n' roll can be as substantive and important as any great art, and that smart, passionate people can devote their lives to exploring and reveling in its many contradictions—between beauty and ugliness, contemplation and aggression, control and chaos, the Dionysian and the Apollonian, love and hate, and life and death.

As with so many aspects of this band, Lester Bangs phrased it best: "Everybody assumes that mind and body are opposed. Why? (Leaving aside six thousand years of history.) The trog vs. the cerebrite. How boring. But we still buy it, all of us. The Velvet Underground were the greatest band that ever existed because they began to suggest that such was not so."

Lou Reed and John Cale collaborated on *Songs for Drella*, a musical biography of Andy Warhol released in 1990.

Several of the numerous Lou Reed, John Cale, and Nico recordings from the Bataclan concerts.

Lou Reed, John Cale, and Nico reunite at the Parisian nightclub Bataclan, January 29, 1972. *Mick Gold/Redferns*

THE ANDY WARHOL MUSEUM

John Cale
Sterling Morrison
Moe Tucker

perform new music
to accompany Andy
Warhol's silent films
Kiss and *Eat*

Friday
November 18

Saturday
November 19, 1994

9 pm

Publicity photograph, c. 1967,
from the archives of The Andy Warhol
Museum, Founding Collection,
Contribution The Andy Warhol Foundation
for the Visual Arts, Inc.

With the opening of the Andy Warhol Museum in Pittsburgh, Pennsylvania, on May 14, 1994, John Cale, Sterling Morrison, and Moe Tucker performed "new music" as soundtracks to two Warhol films.

The 1990s witnessed a renewal of interest in and appreciation of the Velvet Underground. Box set of images and recordings from a 1990 German museum exhibit, *Pop Goes Art: Andy Warhol & Velvet Underground.*

Robert Quine's tapes of the Velvets from three 1969 concerts were released in 2001 as *Bootleg Series Volume 1: The Quine Tapes.*

Peel Slowly and See, the five-disc box set, including early band demos, was released on September 26, 1995.

Under the headline "Revival of the Hippest," *New Musical Express* highlighted the Velvet Underground reunion, June 5, 1993.

Art poster, European Reunion Tour, 1993. *Artist: Alessandro Locchi*

Backstage pass, 1993 European Reunion Tour.

The Velvet Underground members take the stage during their 1993 European Reunion Tour. *Leon Morris/Redferns*

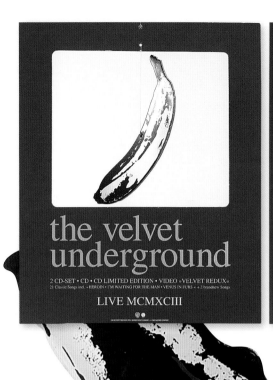
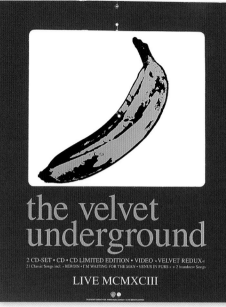

Hanging mobile promoting *Live MCMXCIII*. Collection Michael E. Fields/Mick Black

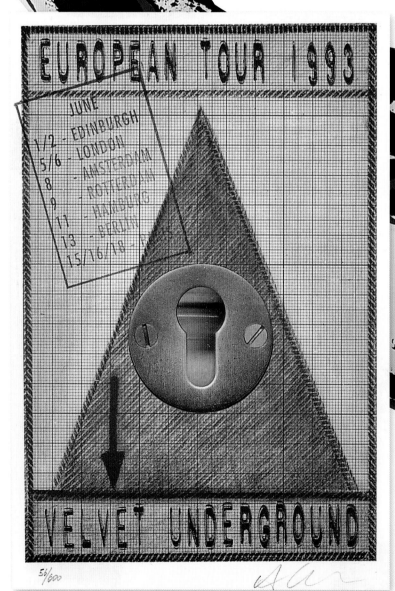

Hologram handbill, European Reunion Tour, 1993.
Artist: Alessandro Locchi

Poster, Die Halle Weissensee, Berlin, Germany, June 20, 1993.
Collection Michael E. Fields/Mick Black

Poster, St. Jakob's Stadion, Basel, Switzerland, June 30, 1993.

Promotional blow-up banana for the release of *Live MCMXCIII*.

rock and

roll

hf

hall of fame

Program, Rock and Roll Hall of Fame Induction, January 17, 1996.

Swallowed Up by the Armadillos: Sterling Speaks

By Bill Bentley

He was sitting at the bar in the Cedar Door, and it was deathly hot outside. Austin's summers were brutal: over one hundred degrees for weeks in a row. Tall, thin, and with a prominent moustache at the time, Sterling Morrison looked like any other graduate student in 1975, wearing a white T-shirt and blue jeans while spending the afternoon with a pitcher of cold beer. He was off on an intense harangue about the awfulness of Frank Zappa, and how the Californian's entire career was fraudulent and unworthy of serious consideration. I listened for a half-hour, and then turned to ask, "Is your name Sterling?" He was shocked. For over a year he'd been going by his Christian name Holmes in the English Department at the University of Texas, where he was working on his doctorate. After a few quick seconds sizing me up, he said simply, "Who wants to know?" It was obvious he was hiding from his past musical notoriety.

That's how I met Holmes Sterling Morrison. I quickly explained I'd been looking for him for more than a year, but

The Velvet Underground photographed in the Factory, with Sterling Morrison on the couch in the foreground. *Nat Finkelstein*

no one would introduce us. A few of his fellow grad students had told me, "You don't want to meet him." But I did. I was an absolute acolyte of the Velvet Underground, and I needed to know everything. When I asked Morrison if he would do an interview for the weekly newspaper the *Austin Sun*, he said he'd think about. I gave him my phone number, and we then proceeded to drink the rest of the afternoon away.

Morrison had left the Velvet Underground in August 1971, right after appearances in Houston and right before the beginning of a European tour. He had liked Austin when the Velvets played here in 1969 at the Vulcan Gas Company, and he decided the seventies would be a good time to continue his academic endeavors. At the time of our meeting, Morrison was taking the orals for his Ph.D. in English literature, teaching a sophomore English section, and, oddly enough, a course in J.R.R. Tolkien at the University of Texas.

Three weeks later, Morrison called to arrange the interview. We talked for three hours, and I realized he'd barely scratched the surface. When I turned the story in to my editor, he read it and immediately offered his opinion: "It's too smart for Austin. People here won't get it." Exactly.

Soon after the story was published, on October 19, 1975, Sterling Morrison and I were friends, and I began cajoling him to join our bar band the Bizarros. It took a year, but when it happened, I felt like I'd hit the jackpot. He brought out his Fender Stratocaster with the most beautiful leather guitar strap in existence, but even better than his rhythm guitar playing was Morrison's company. One of the smartest people I've ever met, he also was a monologist of the highest order, an expert on every subject under the sun, even if it was all based on sheer bravado and his unrelenting way with words. Sterling never stopped talking, and he was almost always right. I used to say I graduated from V.U.—that's how voluminous his memories were of the Velvet Underground.

Unfortunately, in 1979, Sterling decided I should be punished for a deed not of my doing, and I was given his cold shoulder for the next ten years. We finally fixed the split in Paris when the Velvets went there as part of the Cartier Foundation's Andy Warhol exhibition. I was Lou

Reed's press rep, and those three days still seem like a dream. The band performed an unplanned but volatile version of "Heroin" at the event, and as I watched Sterling recall the chords from all those years ago, I suddenly realized my face was all wet under a perfectly dry sky. Luckily, I got to tell him I loved him over the telephone two days before he died. By then, he could no longer speak, but the soft groan he answered me with might be the sweetest sound I've ever heard.

I miss Holmes Sterling Morrison every day, still not knowing how I had the great good fortune to become his friend. I'll never meet anyone remotely like him again. These words from that interview in 1975 are only a small window into his vast mind, but they'll have to do. He used to look at me sometimes with that intensely inquisitive stare and say, "You know, we don't have to worry; we're Catholics. We're going to heaven." Save me a spot, Sterling. I forgot to ask the name of your Ludlow Street roommate who wallpapered the entire living room with one-cent stamps.

I once read that before the Velvet Underground began, the first bands were called the Falling Spikes, then the Warlocks. What were those?

MORRISON: Those were jokes. We would call ourselves one thing one night and another thing another. Whoever would show up played. Earlier, when Lou and I were at Syracuse, we would change our name at least once a week. We were playing for fraternities, and they wanted Top Ten music. We didn't know any; all we knew was Jimmy Reed songs and all that. Then the word began to get out, "Don't hire these turkeys." So we would change our name again. Before they knew it, it was too late. L.A. and the Eldorados, Pasha and the Prophets, Moses and His Brothers—it was outrageous.

Where had you met Lou Reed?

At Syracuse University. A few of us were playing Lightnin' Hopkins records at four o'clock in the morning, and he lived upstairs and came down and knocked on our door and asked if he could listen. It was an accident.

What happened after Syracuse?

I was there less than a year. Later, I saw Lou and Cale in the subway in New York. They said they were going to the East Side to listen to records and maybe play some. I went along, got high, and started making some noise. From there is how I ended up at Pickwick City.

Pickwick City?

A record company on Long Island. We worked there and were songwriters on occasion. Pickwick did those supermarket albums where you never know who's playing. At one time, they called us the Beachnuts. Lou did one notable song called "Cycle Annie," about a girl who had a motorcycle and rode her boyfriend around on the back. Some psychologist heard the thing and wrote a little treatise on it saying the

song showed sexual inversion and role reversal and all that sort of thing. When we finally quit there, that was it. Everyone was retiring: no more music. That's when we started writing "Heroin" and those songs. We decided if we weren't going to play anymore, we could begin to just amuse ourselves. Cale had already given up on serious music: He lasted two weeks at Tanglewood and quit.

Why had Cale come to the U.S.?

He'd won a Leonard Bernstein Fellowship. John was voted the Best Young Composer in Europe in 1965. Aaron Copland was his sponsor. So they brought him over, and after two weeks at Tanglewood, he had a big falling out with [Tanglewood Music Director Erich] Leinsdorf and said, "Ah, screw you." Then he worked with John Cage and La Monte Young. He stumbled into Pickwick one day to play a session, and Lou said, "Hey, what's the story? Let's do something."

When the Velvet Underground began, was there a feeling of alienation from the music world?

No, not really. We started out from a condition of retirement, so we just wanted to do the songs that pleased us.

What was your reaction to the early criticism that the band members weren't accomplished musicians?

We thought it was funny. All we had to do was push Cale forward, and he had the best credentials of anybody I ever heard of. "These people have no talent. They aren't musicians. They must be some people Warhol found in the street and propped up onstage." What a joke.

Where had you met Warhol?

Andy heard us once, probably by accident, at the Café Bizarre. I remember Gerard Malanga had come there with a whip; he was probably on his way to the Factory for a movie. Anyway, he was on the dance floor, swinging this huge whip around. I was thinking, "Who is this lunatic?" It turned out to be Gerard. Then, after seeing us, Andy wined and dined us. He had booked two weeks at the Cinemathèque and wanted to have dancing and films, and he also wanted a band. He knew we had all these strange songs and a strange name and asked us to be the band. We said, "What do we have to do?" Andy said, "Just play music." Those nights at the Cinemathèque I consider the first performances for a real audience, for people who ultimately were the ones we wanted to reach.

What was Warhol's contribution to the band?

He was mainly there with encouragement and reinforcement when we first got the hostile press attacks. We had already retired to begin with, so it would have been easy to go out and get a bad review and go back to what we were doing before: not playing in public. We didn't have that much self-confidence. But Andy said, "Don't worry about it, it's all right. Just keep doing what you are doing. People have their own angles. It doesn't matter what you're doing, they are going to make it into what they want it to be." That really did help. He convinced us to keep doing what we were doing, and also that there is no such thing as bad publicity.

Did he like the music?

Yes, but I don't think he pays that much attention to music. There are things about lyrics that he likes, and things about performance that he likes. He loves excitement, but I don't think he analyzes music. There were other people around who were more than willing to do that—the whole Factory crew. I'd say that of everybody at the Factory, Andy had the least true appreciation of music. He just liked what he liked and didn't pay attention to the rest. His appreciation was of the effect of certain things happening onstage, and the excitement in general.

What were the first performances like? What went on?

Everything. The dancers could do what they liked, the film people could do whatever they liked, and we could do whatever we liked. The first night we played "Heroin" there, two people fainted. That is one of my rock memories. This girl leaped up and started clapping hysterically and, boom, she's out. I wasn't sure if it was drugs or emotion. The audiences then were wild—climbing-the-rafters wild. There was complete spillover from audience to stage. A lot of people came out of the audience to go on to superstardom.

Why was "Heroin" written?

We wanted to write an honest drug song. There was only one drug song we had ever heard, and that was "Cocaine Blues." The lines were, "Cocaine's for horses but not for men/They say it'll kill you, but they don't say when." Big joke: ha, ha, ha, right? What bullshit. Lou wrote the lyric to "Heroin." He was home, captured by his parents, and that's what he was doing. Then John and I totally changed the song.

How important were drugs to the Velvet Underground?

They were just there; we didn't make a secret about them, that's all. It is part of the everyday experience of millions. Some of my best friends took drugs, as the saying goes. Seems like all of them did.

What came next?

Let's see. . . After we moved to the Factory, we rented the Dom, which was an old Polish dance hall. This was before there was an "East Village." Then, it was just where old people and poor people lived. The Dom can be credited with making St. Mark's Place the sleaze hole that it is today. It was the first "hip" invasion. We wanted to have our own place so nobody could tell us what to do. It was a huge success. Then, while we were in California, playing and recording, the notorious criminal Albert Grossman had our landlord tear up the lease and

give the hall to him. He renamed it the Balloon Farm; later, it became the Electric Circus.

When you came back from California and the Dom wasn't yours, what did you do?

We went back to the Factory and didn't do anything. Andy said, "Oh, gee, wouldn't it be nice if you were playing somewhere?" We had no agent, and Andy was our manager, but he had no idea at all about how to go about it. We didn't have a record company, either, though we had done some recording in California, using the money we had made at the Dom.

You felt like you needed to record?

Well, groups are supposed to have records.

Was it odd to be recording songs like "Heroin" and "Venus In Furs" and "I'm Waiting For The Man"?

We knew then that was the reason no record company would sign us up front. This was the "two minute, thirty second era." The first album was truly revolutionary, and I knew it at the time. Beyond lyrics, beyond instrumentation, beyond anything—just the fact that the songs did not last two minutes, thirty seconds. "Heroin" lasts over seven minutes, because that is how long it takes to play. That was the first rock album to break out of that format.

How did you end up signed with MGM?

At first we took our tapes around to everyone. Jack Holzman of Elektra told us we had to clean up the sound, but we wanted the feedback and the drones, so that was no good. Ahmet Ertegun at Atlantic said, "No 'Heroin' and no 'Venus In Furs.'" We had to have those songs, so that didn't work. Finally, MGM, who have no conception of rock music and probably never even listened to our albums—or if they did, it was with very little comprehension—said we could do anything we wanted. After signing, MGM shafted us, too. The first album was complete as a package and ready to go in early '66 but wasn't released until late in the year. It was sabotaged so Zappa and the Mothers' first album *Freak Out!* could be issued before ours. Zappa's was two albums for the price of one, and ours was one album for the price of two, because of the banana. Then there was a lawsuit right after it was released that took it out of circulation.

What was the lawsuit about?

Eric Emerson sued MGM. The original jacket had an upside-down picture of Eric in the light show with his arms spread, encircling the band. One day, Eric gets busted with ten thousand doses of acid, needs money, and walks up to MGM and says, "You're using my picture illegally, so I'm going to sue you." The company was so fucking stupid, they took the record off the market. In a million years, Eric couldn't have won that lawsuit, but MGM just freaked. Later, another jacket was printed with Eric's image clouded out.

Was Warhol's banana painting on the cover a hindrance to being heard primarily as a rock band?

We had a little trouble getting accepted anyway. Having Andy do the cover was just natural. He went to Sam Goody Record Store on Broadway to look at record jackets and decided white was the best color. There were pictures but not promo blurbs or credits or anything on the outside. Plus, the quotes on the inside from the critics were mostly negative. Originally, they were all negative, but MGM included some positive quotes. We gathered the worst things that had been said about us and stuck them in. We thought that any schmuck who is more motivated by reading reviews than by listening to the music, well, here it is, all sitting here, telling him how bad it is. Someone goes out and buys this thing, God knows motivated by what, and then opens it up and reads how bad it is. We had a good time with that.

How accurate was the drug image?

Accurate.

Do you think it hurt the band?

No, it just happened. You can't control those things—even though we didn't do anything to help it out in those days, either, being sinister and all. I didn't want to be known as a gay band, though. I certainly didn't care for that association, which I guess was absorbed from Warhol. It took a while to dispel that image. A lot of associations come from a lot of different places, not all of them accurate.

Did the associations have any repercussions in your acceptance?

Sure. The thing I'm most pissed about is that we were banned in New York for three years, '66 to '69, inclusive. Right up front, we were excluded from any FM radio play. AM was already out of the question: no music and no advertising. In our home city, the media capital of Earth, the native sons are banned. You compare that to San Francisco, where the mayor is kissing the ass of Big Brother & the Holding Company, and they've become a part of the city life and a tourist attraction and all.

What was the ban about?

Our lyrics were "objectionable." Since the radio refused to play us, we retaliated by refusing all jobs in New York. From '67 to '70, we didn't play in New York, except for private parties, and once at Lincoln Center. And even Pacifica Radio, the supposed non-commercial station, joined in the ban. In the beginning, they were the only FM airplay we got. They always told us, "You and the Fugs are the real people—real community bands." Then once they were having a benefit at Tompkins Square Park to raise a bail fund. We were very much

known for playing benefits: We always did. Pacifica approached us to play and we thought, "Sure, why not. It's just around the corner from where we live." Then we asked them, "By the way, who's the benefit for?" They said, "The people who get busted for grass and acid." We thought that was kind of curious. We asked them, "What about the people busted for junk and speed?" They said, "Oh, no, those are bad drugs." How idiotic. Bad drugs—all of a sudden there are "bad drugs." We told them either they bail everybody out, or we don't play. Word got back to the head of the Pacifica station, who then said we were horrible people, blah, blah, blah, not supporting community efforts and so on. We told them that our notion of community is evidently more complete than his. The result was that the ban was complete: a total blackout in New York City. Our altruism got in the way of our airplay. Any success in New York was through television and newspapers. It had nothing to do with the legitimate outlet, which is radio. The music simply was not heard. To think that some self-righteous creep was saying yes to grass and acid but no to junk and speed really infuriated us. Who knows? It may be that all drugs are bad. But if some people get bailed out, let's bail everybody out.

Why did Cale leave the band?

John was getting very flamboyant. His girlfriend [designer Betsey Johnson] was dressing him, and he was really shaping up as a performer, playing very energetically. Then Lou just got uptight. There was some kind of collision. Lou found me one night and said, "Here's what's happening: The band is dissolved. I'm going to put together another band called the Velvet Underground and you can be in it if you want to be, and Maureen, and we'll find somebody else." I shouldn't have gone for that, but I might have been slightly corrupted at that point. Mainly I wanted to keep playing the songs that I'd worked so hard on.

What kind of person was your drummer Maureen?

Clever, enigmatic, feminine—which at that point meant that she was pushed around. She was not the big bull dyke some people thought she was; exactly the opposite. She sort of rolled with the punches and let all the major arguing be done by Lou, John, and me.

When Lou left in 1970, was there a major breakdown?

To this day, I can't give you any explanation why Lou left. And he can't either. I thought he had gone insane—gone insane in a very dull way. I have my own evidence. He suddenly went home to Freeport and decided to become reconciled with his parents. The only conversations they ever had were their threats to have him committed and his counter-threats and what not. Lou usually went home when he had hepatitis or was about to die. When he left in '70, when we were finishing our job at Max's, it was like his parents had come and claimed him and took him away. Lou was unstable in such a tedious way. It wasn't that he was running around crazy in the streets; at times, he was incommunicative and remote and content to stay with his parents.

When you quit in '71, what were your reasons?

I have all sorts of reasons, but one is that there were no good places left to play. That was the one thing that was upsetting; it was upsetting all through 1970. All the big old ballrooms were closing. You were left with only two kinds of performances: Either you did small clubs, where you couldn't get any decent sound out of your amplifiers because the place was too small and you'd blow the roof off, or else you had to do stand up/sit down concerts. The band stands up, and the audience sits and watches. I never liked doing those, and we had done enough of them, so I really knew. That was when rock 'n' roll was propelled into theater. By that time, we had divorced ourselves from the theatrical, and had disbanded the Exploding Inevitable. When everybody else had lights shows, there was no point in our still doing it. All we were going to do was play music. When you get on a stage or huge concert hall where everybody is sitting down, they're not going to do anything but sit on their ass, so you have to do everything. The scope of it, the height and width and depth of the stage, demands that something fill it up: props, dancing, or whatever. Some zaniness. That is why the size of bands is burgeoning: Something had to fill up that space. This is the reason the Rolling Stones are doing what they're doing. If anybody could stand on just the music, you would

think they could, but they can't. They have to build those sets and the phalluses and the whole thing. We had the choice of going back into something that we felt we had already gone beyond: the theatrics. It was nice to be there at the very beginning; we did do it when it was new and creative and exciting, but to go back and do it because you have to, that was different.

Was there a time when the Velvets decided they weren't going to push for commercial success?

We always wanted to be commercially successful, but on our own terms. We wanted to do the music we were doing, and we hoped that tastes would change—or that we could change tastes. That is what everybody felt in the sixties. That is what the whole psychedelic thing was about: AM vs. FM. We thought, the Grateful Dead thought, the Airplane, everybody thought we could obliterate AM radio. Change it forever. But it didn't happen, it really didn't happen. If anything, it's gone the other way.

In the beginning, was there a single factor that the band shared?

We always took the music seriously. The idea that you could do something on your own terms, I found that facet peculiar. That was strange. I couldn't really anticipate being able to do that.

Was it fun?

Great fun. What could be more fun that that: being able to do exactly what you want to do?

What were the highlights for you?

All the early things that happened impressed me mightily. Highlights to me always turn out to be live performances, places I played. I never felt like the records did what they ought to do; they were never the way I dreamed they should be. I guess the first album is the one I'm most proud of. A few cuts here and there on the others. And *Loaded*, the last album. Dougie [Yule] and I pretty much had the say on that. One producer went crazy during the recording of *Loaded*, Adrian Barber. Freedom drove him mad. But live performances are what I loved.

How did you end up at the University of Texas?

I wanted to get my Ph.D. The Velvet Underground for me was like a crusade to get the music played and appreciated. We sort of accomplished that. And even though it was still fun, near the end, it wasn't the same.

What did your friends say when you quit the band?

Well, Warhol said it was the right thing to do, that it would be good for me. But most of them said, "Sterling, you know, he went to Texas." And that's it—like I was swallowed up by the armadillos.

The Velvet Underground and Nico pose for an image planned for the banana album cover.
Billy Name/OvoWorks, Inc.

LIVE PERFORMANCES 1971–1973

BY OLIVIER LANDEMAINE

January 1971: The Alpine, North Conway, NH. Week-long engagement.

January 29–30, 1971: Electric Circus, New York City

February 3–6, 1971: The Alpine, North Conway, NH

April 28, 1971: The Agora, Columbus, OH

May 5, 1971: The Music Palace, Saint Louis, MO

May 1971: Cleveland, OH

May 8, 1971: Palladium, Birmingham, MI

June 1971: Gloucester, MA

June 15, 1971: Palladium, Birmingham, MI

June 18, 1971: Vanity Ballroom, Detroit, MI

June 24–27, 1971: Main Point, Philadelphia, PA

July 10, 1971: The Park, Baltimore, OH

August 20–21, 1971: Liberty Hall, Houston, TX

August 1971: Aquarius Club, Revere, MA

September 3, 1971: The Vanity Ballroom, Detroit, MI

September 6, 1971: The Park, Baltimore, OH

September 17, 1971: Pacific Coliseum, Vancouver, British Columbia, Canada

September 18, 1971: Jasper Place Arena, Edmonton, Alberta, Canada

October 8, 1971: Birmingham University, Birmingham, U.K.

October 9, 1971: Kingston Polytechnic, Kingston-Upon-Thames, U.K.

October 10, 1971: Concertgebouw, Amsterdam, The Netherlands

October 11, 1971: AVRO Studio, Hilversum, The Netherlands. TV appearance.

October 1971: Speakeasy Club, London, U.K.

October 14, 1971: London College of Printing, London, U.K.

October 15, 1971: Reading University, Reading, U.K.

October 16, 1971: Dagenham Roundhouse, London, U.K.

October 20, 1971: Strathclyde University, Glasgow, Scotland

October 21, 1971: Warwick University, Warwick, U.K.

October 22, 1971: Southampton University, Southampton, U.K.

October 23, 1971: Manchester University, Manchester, U.K.

October 26, 1971: St John's College, Oxford, U.K.

October 28, 1971: Bristol University, Bristol, U.K.

October 29, 1971: Lancaster University, Lancaster, U.K.

October 30, 1971: Liverpool University, Liverpool, U.K.

November 2, 1971: South Parade Pier, Southsea, U.K.

November 4, 1971: Kent University, Canterbury, U.K.

November 5, 1971: School of African and Oriental Studies, London, U.K.

November 6, 1971: Leeds University, Leeds, U.K.

November 11, 1971: Gray's Technical College, U.K.

November 12, 1971: Town Hall, Aylesbury, U.K.

November 13, 1971: Hull University, Hull, U.K.

November 14, 1971: Bumpers Club, London, U.K.

November 19, 1971: Concertgebouw, Amsterdam, The Netherlands

November 20, 1971: Ergens In Nederland, The Netherlands

November 21, 1971: Concertzaal de Jong, Groningen, The Netherlands

November 18, 1972: Malvern Winter Gardens, London, U.K.

November 20, 1972: Top Rank, Doncaster, U.K.

November 22, 1972: Acton Town Hall, London, U.K.

November 26, 1972: Top Rank, Cardiff, Wales

December 2, 1972: City Hall, St Albans, U.K.

December 4, 1972: Reading Suite, Reading, U.K.

December 6, 1972: St David's University, Lampeter, Wales

December 9, 1972: Northamptonshire Cricket Club, Northampton, U.K.

May 1973: Oliver's, Boston, MA, and New England tour. The final appearances as the Velvet Underground. As Doug Yule told *Mojo* in February 2000: "There was a cover band in 1973—me and my brother and two other guys, doing rock 'n' roll tunes both Velvet Underground and non–Velvet Underground, and some original tunes. We met somebody who started booking us around New England. He was supposed to bill us as featuring me from the Velvet Underground, but he wasn't supposed to say it was the Velvet Underground. We played next to [Boston's] Fenway Park in Kenmore Square, probably our second-to-last show. The last show was some ski-place in Vermont or someplace; we drove in, saw 'The Velvet Underground' and said, 'That's the last straw.' Plus, the place turned out to be a real dive. It was one of those places you hear (*in whining voices*) 'Can you turn it down? Can you play Louie, Louie?' We didn't even play the second night; the guy asked us to leave."

REUNION PERFORMANCES

1972–1996

January 29, 1972: Le Bataclan, Paris, France. The concert was also shown on TV and featured John Cale, Nico, and Lou Reed.

December 3, 1989: Brooklyn Academy of Music, Brooklyn, NY. Performance of *Songs for Drella* featuring Cale, Reed, and Tucker.

June 15, 1990: Fondation Cartier, Jouy-En-Josas, France. "Andy Warhol System: Pub, Pop, Rock" exhibition opening, featuring Cale, Morrison, Reed, and Tucker.

February 20, 1992: Casino de Paris, Paris, France. Featuring Tucker, Morrison, and Reed.

December 5, 1992: New York University, New York City. Featuring Cale, Morrison, and Reed.

June 1–2, 1993: The Playhouse, Edinburgh, Scotland. First shows of the 1993 European Reunion Tour.

June 5, 1993: The Forum, London, U.K.

June 6, 1993: Wembley Arena, London, U.K.

June 8, 1993: Paradiso, Amsterdam, The Netherlands

June 9, 1993: Ahoy Sportpaleis, Rotterdam, The Netherlands

June 11, 1993: Alsterdorfer Sporthalle, Hamburg, Germany

June 13, 1993: Palàc Kultury, Praze, Czech Republic. President Vaclav Havel in attendance.

June 15–17, 1993: L'Olympia, Paris, France

June 20, 1993: Die Halle Weissensee, Berlin, Germany

June 23, 1993: Stade de la Meinau, Strasbourg, France

June 25, 1993: Glastonbury Festival, Pilton, U.K.

June 26, 1993: Hippodrome de Vincennes, Paris, France

June 28, 1993: Stade de la Pontaise, Lausanne, Switzerland

June 30, 1993: St. Jakob's Stadion, Basel, Switzerland

July 2, 1993: Roskilde Festival, Roskilde, Denmark

July 4, 1993: Villa Manin, Udine, Italy

July 6, 1993: Arena Parco Nord, Bologna, Italy

July 7, 1993: Forum Assago, Milano

July 9, 1993: Stadio San Paolo, Napoli, Italy

November 18–19, 1994: Andy Warhol Museum, Pittsburgh, PA. Featuring Cale, Morrison, and Tucker performing music to accompany Andy Warhol's silent films *Eat* and *Kiss*.

January 17, 1996: Rock and Roll Hall of Fame Induction dinner, the Waldorf Astoria, New York City. Featuring Cale, Reed, and Tucker, the band performed "Last Night I Said Goodbye To My Friend" in honor of Morrison.

WHAT BECOMES A LEGEND MOST? (WELL BABY TONIGHT IT'S YOU)

The Velvet Underground and Nico
A Symphony of Sound

ALL TOMORROW'S PARTIES

REMEMBERING
THE VELVET UNDERGROUND

THE VELVET UNDERGROUND

1990

LOU REED
SOME KINDA LOVE

Lou Reed

Hero & Heroine

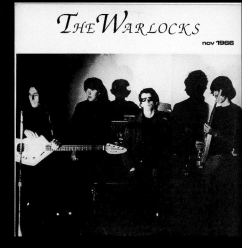

THE WARLOCKS

nov 1966

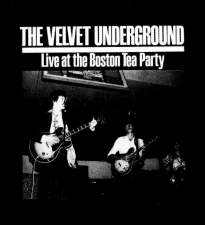

THE VELVET UNDERGROUND
Live at the Boston Tea Party

LIVE '68

20. 6. 93 BERLIN - DIE HALLE

The
Velvet Underground
Story

VELVET UNDERGROUND
LIVE IN AMSTERDAM

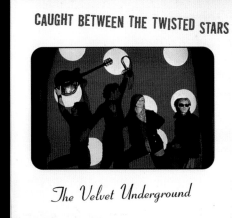

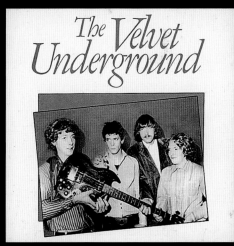

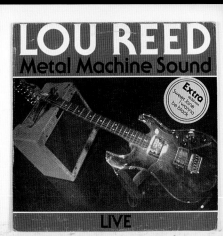

"the velvet underground -etc."

"the velvet underground (and so on)"

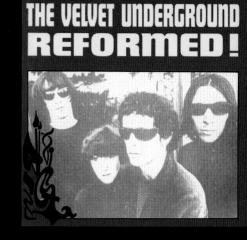

THE VELVET UNDERGROUND REFORMED!

VELVET UNDERGROUND

JUNE 1, 1993
THE PLAYHOUSE, EDINBURGH, SCOTLAND

THE VELVET UNDERGROUND

EVEN MORE VENGEANCE

VELVET UNDERGROUND
LIVE USA '93

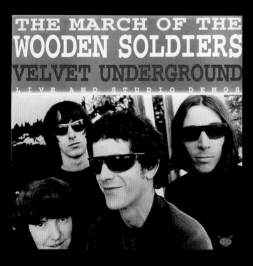

THE MARCH OF THE WOODEN SOLDIERS
VELVET UNDERGROUND
LIVE AND STUDIO DEMOS

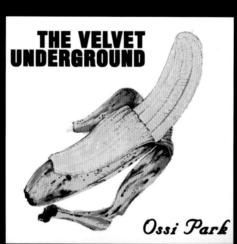

THE VELVET UNDERGROUND

Ossi Park

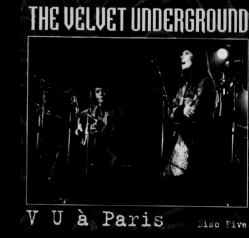

Andy Warhol

THE VELVET UNDERGROUND

So Blue   Disc One & Two

THE VELVET UNDERGROUND

Afterhours   Disc Three & Four

THE VELVET UNDERGROUND

V U à Paris   Disc Five

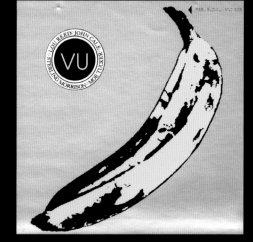

Evil Mothers — RARE VELVETS

SKYDOG LP 003

INCLUDES UNRELEASED LIVE TRACKS AND RARE LOU REED ORIGINALS

VELVET UNDERGROUND
Harvest '93

Campbell's
CONDENSED

BANANA
FRUIT

The Velvet Underground
The Lost Live Tapes 1969

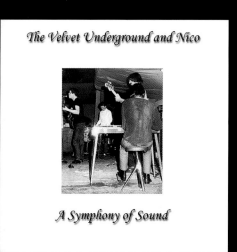

The Velvet Underground and Nico

A Symphony of Sound

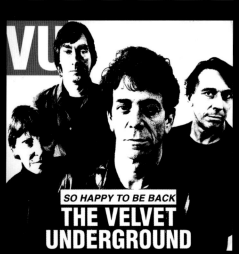

VU

SO HAPPY TO BE BACK
THE VELVET
UNDERGROUND

VELVET
UNDERGROUND

SWEET SISTER RAY'S MURDER MYSTERY

THE VELVET UNDERGROUND/LA CAVE 1968
P R O B L E M S   I N   U R B A N   L I V I N G

VELVET

TAKE A TRIP

UNDERGROUND

THE
VELVET
UNDERGROUND

WITH US FROM THE PAST

ACKNOWLEDGMENTS

Our thanks, in alphabetical order, to Charles Bilz; Greg Burchard at the Andy Warhol Museum; Bob Driscoll; Michael E. Fields/Mick Black; Nat and Elizabeth Finkelstein; Asako Kitaori and Gerard Malanga; Kevin Kushell and Billy Name; Olivier Landemaine; Lisa Law and Pilar Law; Alessandro Locchi; Ian MacEachern; Gloria McDarrah; Rick McGrath; Michael Randolph; Stephen Shore and Laura Steele; Maureen Tucker; and Wes Wilson.

DISCOGRAPHY

BY OLIVIER LANDEMAINE

Any discography of the Velvet Underground is an opportunity for confusion and contention. And this only seems befitting for the band. There are multiple versions of most original releases, including mono versus stereo versions, "lawsuit" issues, DJ and other promotional copies, reissues, repackaged versions, pirated and bootlegged versions, and a multitude of variations released around the globe. This discography focuses on the original U.S. home-market releases only, including greatest hits and reissues released during the band's prime years. It does not include the myriad reissues, collections, boxed sets, and so on, nor does it include that most contentious of releases, the *Squeeze* LP by the "Velveteen Underground." For a thorough discography of American as well as international versions and their many variants, including bootlegs, see Olivier Landemaine's phenomenal online discography at http://olivier.landemaine.free.fr/vu/.

LPs

The Velvet Underground & Nico

Verve V-5008 (mono), V6-5008 (stereo)
Released March 1967
Produced by Andy Warhol. Edited and remixed under the supervision of Tom Wilson by Gene Radice and David Greene. Recording engineers: Omi Haden—T.T.G. Hollywood. Director of engineering: Val Valentin.

SIDE 1
1. Sunday Morning
2. I'm Waiting For The Man
3. Femme Fatale
4. Venus In Furs
5. Run Run Run
6. All Tomorrow's Parties

SIDE 2
7. Heroin
8. There She Goes Again
9. I'll Be Your Mirror
10. The Black Angel's Death Song
11. European Son

White Light/White Heat

Verve V-5046 (mono), V6-5046 (stereo)
Released January 30, 1968
Produced by Tom Wilson. Recording engineer: Gary Kellgren. Director of engineering: Val Valentin.

SIDE 1
1. White Light/White Heat
2. The Gift
3. Lady Godiva's Operation
4. Here She Comes Now

SIDE 2
5. I Heard Her Call My Name
6. Sister Ray

The Velvet Underground

MGM SE-4617 (stereo)
Released March 1969
Director of engineering: Val Valentin.

SIDE 1
1. Candy Says
2. What Goes On
3. Some Kinda Love
4. Pale Blue Eyes
5. Jesus

SIDE 2
6. Beginning To See The Light
7. I'm Set Free
8. That's The Story Of My Life
9. The Murder Mystery
10. Afterhours

Loaded

Cotillion SD 9034

Released September 1970

Recording engineers: Adrian Barber & Geoffrey Haslam. Re-mix engineer: Geoffrey Haslam. Production: Geoffrey Haslam, Shel Kagan & the Velvet Underground.

SIDE 1

1. Who Loves The Sun
2. Sweet Jane
3. Rock & Roll
4. Cool It Down
5. New Age

SIDE 2

6. Head Held High
7. Lonesome Cowboy Bill
8. I Found A Reason
9. Train Round The Bend
10. Oh! Sweet Nuthin'

Live At Max's Kansas City

Cotillion SD 9500 (mono)

Released May 30, 1972

Recording: Brigid Polk. Editing and production supervision: Geoff Haslam. Album coordination: Mark Meyerson.

SIDE 1

1. I'm Waiting For The Man
2. Sweet Jane
3. Lonesome Cowboy Bill
4. Beginning To See The Light

SIDE 2

5. I'll Be Your Mirror
6. Pale Blue Eyes
7. Sunday Morning
8. New Age
9. Femme Fatale
10. Afterhours

Lou Reed and The Velvet Underground: That's The Story Of My Life

Pride PRD-0022

Released 1973

Greatest-hits collection.

SIDE 1

1. That's The Story Of My Life
2. Sister Ray
3. Lady Godiva's Operation

SIDE 2

4. Heroin
5. Sunday Morning
6. All Tomorrow's Parties
7. There She Goes Again
8. White Light/White Heat
9. Femme Fatale

1969: The Velvet Underground Live with Lou Reed

Mercury SRM 2-7504

Released September 1974

A and R: Paul Nelson. Mastering: Gilbert Kong.

SIDE 1

1. Waiting For My Man
2. Lisa Says
3. What Goes On
4. Sweet Jane

SIDE 2

5. We're Gonna Have A Real Good Time Together
6. Femme Fatale
7. New Age
8. Rock & Roll
9. Beginning To See The Light

SIDE 3

10. Ocean
11. Pale Blue Eyes
12. Heroin

SIDE 4

13. Some Kinda Love
14. Over You
15. Sweet Bonnie Brown/It's Just Too Much
16. White Light/White Heat
17. I'll Be Your Mirror

VU

Verve Polygram 823 721-1 Y-1

Released February 1985

"A collection of previously unreleased recordings." All recordings originally produced by the Velvet Underground. Recordings mixed June 1984 except "Ocean," mixed June 1969. Executive producer: Bill Levenson. Mixed and engineered by Michael Barbiero.

SIDE 1
1. I Can't Stand It
2. Stephanie Says
3. She's My Best Friend
4. Lisa Says
5. Ocean

SIDE 2
6. Foggy Notion
7. Inside Your Heart
8. One Of These Days
9. Andy's Chest
10. I'm Sticking With You

Another View
Verve Polygram 829 405-1 Y-1
Released September 1986
"A collection of previously unreleased recordings." Originally produced and arranged by the Velvet Underground. Executive producer: Bill Levenson. Engineer: J. C. Convertino.

SIDE 1
1. We're Gonna Have A Real Good Time Together
2. I'm Gonna Move Right In
3. Mr. Rain (Version I)
4. Ride Into The Sun
5. Coney Island Steeplechase

SIDE 2
6. Guess I'm Falling In Love (Instrumental Version)
7. Hey Mr. Rain (Version II)
8. Ferryboat Bill
9. Rock & Roll (Original Version)

Singles and EPs

"All Tomorrow's Parties"/"I'll Be Your Mirror"
> *Verve VK-10427 (mono)*
> *Released July 1966*

"Sunday Morning"/"Femme Fatale"
> *Verve VK-10466 (mono)*
> *Released December 1966*

"White Wind" (by Peter Walker)/"Loop"
> *7-inch flexi-disc, Americom NYC (mono)*
> *Released December 1966*
> *Part of the December 1966 issue of* Aspen *magazine. The label states that "Loop" is "Guitar and feedback," "First half of a 15-minute recording made with two monaural tape recorders." The credits went to John Cale, who is supposedly the only person playing. The flexi has a closed-groove ending so the last groove repeats itself ad infinitum.*

untitled (aka index)
> *7-inch cardboard-disc (mono)*
> *Released February 1967*
> *One-sided picture-disc (featuring a portrait of Lou Reed by Billy Name on the play side), part of Andy Warhol's* Index *book, a multimedia package. It offers the recording of some Factory regulars talking and reacting to the book. The Velvet Underground & Nico album can be heard in the background.*

"White Light/White Heat"/"Here She Comes Now"
> *Verve VK-10560 (mono)*
> *Released November 1967*

"What Goes On"/"Jesus"
> *MGM K-14057 (mono)*
> *Released March 1969*
> *Yellow MGM label, "SPECIAL DISC JOCKEY RECORD"*

The Velvet Underground
> *MGM VU-1 (mono)*
> *Released 1969*
> *Yellow MGM label, "SPECIAL DISC JOCKEY RECORD" Both sides offer a radio ad for the third album, read by Bill "Rosko" Mercer with song excerpts.*

"Who Loves The Sun"/"Oh! Sweet Nuthin'"
> *Cotillion 44107 (mono)*
> *Released April 1971*

"Who Loves The Sun"/"Who Loves The Sun"
> *Cotillion 44107 (mono/stereo)*
> *Released April 1971*

"Foggy Notion" (edit)/"I Can't Stand It"
> *Verve/Polygram PRO 349-1 (stereo)*
> *Released February 1985*

CONTRIBUTOR BIOGRAPHIES

BILL BENTLEY is a drummer, writer, deejay, producer, promoter, publicist, and fan. His fascination with the Velvet Underground dates to 1967. Playing together in a bar band in Austin, Texas, Sterling Morrison taught Bentley the VU's rulebook and tested him frequently.

New Zealand–born, South London–based, and oft' wandering **GARTH CARTWRIGHT** is an award-winning journalist and critic who regularly contributes to *The Guardian*, the *Sunday Times*, *fRoots*, and the BBC's website. He is the author of *Princes Amongst Men: Journeys With Gypsy Musicians* and the forthcoming *More Miles Than Money: Journeys In Wild America*.

JIM DeROGATIS (www.jimdero.com) is the pop music critic at the *Chicago Sun-Times*, the cohost of Public Radio's *Sound Opinions* (the world's only rock 'n' roll talk show), and the author of several books about music and culture, including *Let It Blurt: The Life And Times Of Lester Bangs, America's Greatest Rock Critic,* and *Staring at Sound: The True Story of Oklahoma's Fabulous Flaming Lips.* Though he reserves the right to equivocate, if pressed at this moment (as at most), he will emphatically insist that "I Heard Her Call My Name" is the best song in the history of rock 'n' roll.

GLENN KENNY has written about music and film for the *New York Times*, the *Village Voice*, the *New York Daily News*, *Rolling Stone*, *Entertainment Weekly*, *Film Comment*, and other publications. He was the film critic for *Premiere* magazine 1998–2007 and is the editor of the book *A Galaxy Not So Far Away: Writers and Artists on 25 Years of* Star Wars (2002). He lives in Brooklyn.

Don't blame the Velvets, but **GREG KOT** decided to devote his life to music writing after taking a cross-country trip with the *Live 1969* version of "What Goes On" pounding away in the tape deck of a rusted-out Chevrolet Vega. He has been the music critic at the *Chicago Tribune* since 1990 and has authored several books, including *Wilco: Learning How to Die* and *Ripped: How the Wired Generation Revolutionized Music*. With Jim DeRogatis, he also cohosts the nationally syndicated rock 'n' roll talk show *Sound Opinions*. He can be reached at gregkot.com.

Based in Rennes, France, **OLIVIER LANDEMAINE** is the accomplished author and editor of the Velvet Underground Web Page (olivier.landemaine.free.fr/vu/).

ROB O'CONNOR has placed tiny record reviews in the backs of magazines for the past twenty years from his tiny farmhouse in upstate New York. He has written for *Rolling Stone*, where he served as a senior critic, *SPIN*, *Musician*, *Entertainment Weekly*, *Sound & Vision*, *PASTE*, and *Relix*. He has compiled several hundred lists for Yahoo! Music at his "List of the Day" blog and has contributed to *The Trouser Press Guide to '90s Rock*, *Rolling Stone's Alt-Rock-a-Rama*, and *Kill Your Idols*. He once edited the fanzine *Throat Culture*, which sometimes fetches fifteen dollars on eBay.

DAVID SPRAGUE first heard the Velvet Underground at the age of ten, which explains a lot of things. The first? A move to New York City seven years later in search of the forbidden fruit laid out in song after Velvets song and—oh, yeah—a modicum of intellectual nourishment that wasn't available on Cleveland's near west side. Sprague would go on to edit *Creem* magazine, write for such publications as *Variety*, *Spin*, *Rolling Stone*, the New York *Daily News*, and the *Village Voice* and spend undue amounts of time searching out obscure foodstuffs in and around the homestead in Jackson Heights, Queens. "Candy Says" remains Sprague's favorite Velvet Underground song, which explains a few more things, but that's another story altogether.

ANDY WARHOL is Andy Warhol.

INDEX

"IT WILL REPLACE NOTHING,
EXCEPT MAYBE SUICIDE."

—CHER BONO ON THE EXPLODING
PLASTIC INEVITABLE, 1966

"The unanimous opinion was that we were ten
times better live than we were on records."

—Sterling Morrison, 1981

"LOU WAS DEFINITELY POSSESSED BY ROCK & ROLL. HE WAS
DEFINITELY A ROCK & ROLL PUNK STRAIGHT FROM THE BOOKS,
BUT THE BOOKS WERE ONLY WRITTEN TWENTY YEARS LATER."

—TONY CONRAD, QUOTED IN VICTOR BOCKRIS AND
GERARD MALANGA'S *UP-TIGHT*, 1983

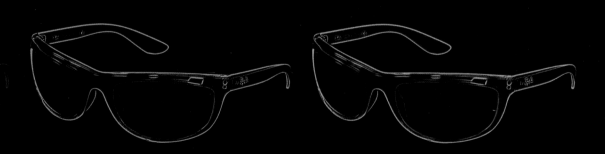

"We weren't just *at* the art exhibit—we *were* the art exhibit,
we were the art incarnate. . . ."